The
BROADWAY
Celebrity
COOKBOOK

Dave and Sharon

"Bon Appetit"

June "92"

The

BROADWAY
Celebrity
COOKBOOK

EDITED BY A.J. VINCENT

Nautilus Books, Inc.
New York

Nautilus Books, Inc.
496 LaGuardia Place
Suite 145
New York, NY 10012

Library of Congress Cataloging-in-Publication Data

The Broadway celebrity cookbook.

    Includes index.
    1. Cookery. 2. Broadway (New York, N.Y.)--
Anecdotes. 3. Theatre--New York (New York, N.Y.)--
Anecdotes. 4. Celebrities--New York (N.Y.)
I. Vincent, A.J., 1958-   .
TX714.B76 1989   641.5   88-34536
ISBN 0-935055-50-9

The information and photographs within have been supplied by the celebrity credited or his/her agent, manager or press associate, unless otherwise noted by the editor. Some editing of recipes, "back burner" stories and biographies has taken place to improve readability and to comply with format. All celebrities were informed by letter of intended use of materials supplied.

First Edition

Printed in the United States of America

10 9 8 7 6 5 4 3 2 1

Cover art ©1989 by David Williams

A heartfelt thanks to the many people who helped make this project cook. I would like to acknowledge: all the celebrities who dug into their recipe boxes and pulled out their favorite dishes; the staff, secretaries, agents and managers of the celebrities; Wallace Munroe and The Actor's Fund of America, Inc. for being such a wonderful, giving organization; Pamela Diedrich for her bravery, David Williams for his creative input; Kathy Kalichman for helping test so many of the recipes; James T. Fitzgerald for his expertise; Lindajean Luca for her careful attention and lifetime of love; my publisher, Eric Perkins, without whom I never could have completed this project; my friends and family for listening to me talk about nothing but food for the past twelve months; and, finally, Bub. Thank you all.

There is no love sincerer than the love of food.
                                        -George Bernard Shaw

The Cast

(in alphabetical order)

EDWARD ASNER

Edward Asner's familiar, gruff face is most recognizable as that of Lou Grant from *The Mary Tyler Moore Show* and *Lou Grant*, and most recently as Joe Danzig, principal of an inner city school on NBC's series, *The Bronx Zoo*. This season, on Broadway, he added the role of Harry Brock in *Born Yesterday* to an already memorable list of professional performances. Also in New York, Mr. Asner appeared with Jack Lemmon in *Face of a Hero*, as Prospero in *The Tempest*, Spinoza in *Venice Preserved* and in the New York and American Shakespeare Festivals. He has countless television and film roles to his credit. He is the recipient of five Golden Globe Awards and seven Emmy Awards for *The Mary Tyler Moore Show*, the ABC mini-series *Roots*, *Rich Man, Poor Man* and his own starring series, *Lou Grant*. He served as National President of The Screen Actors Guild for two terms and is founder of many humanitarian and political organizations working toward peace in Central America, and other human rights groups. His efforts have been recognized with almost twenty awards for distinguished service.

BARBARA BARRIE

Barbara Barrie appeared on Broadway in Stephen Sondheim's *Company, Prisoner of Second Avenue* and *California Suite,* and won the Drama Desk and Obie Awards for her Off-Broadway performance in *Isn't it Romantic.* Also Off-Broadway, Miss Barrie starred in *Beaux' Stratagem, The Crucible, Big and Little, The Killdeer* and worked in three productions for the Public Theatre's Shakespeare in the Park: *Taming of the Shrew, All's Well That Ends Well* and *Twelfth Night.* She received an Oscar nomination for her performance in *Breaking Away,* and the Cannes Film Festival Award for *One Potato, Two Potato.* She also appeared in the films *The Bell Jar, Private Benjamin, End of the Line, Real Men,* and *The Passage.* Television audiences will recognize Miss Barrie from *Barnie Miller, 79 Park Avenue, I'll Take Manhattan, Tucker's Witch* and *Roots II.*

KATHY BATES

Kathy Bates won an Obie Award and a Drama Desk nomination for her critically acclaimed performance as Frankie in Terrence McNally's *Frankie and Johnnie in the Clair de Lune*. She is perhaps best known for her portrayal of the suicidal daughter in Marsha Norman's Pulitzer Prize-winning drama *'night Mother*, for which she won a Tony Award nomination and the Outer Critics' Circle Award. Also on Broadway, she appeared in *Fifth of July* and *Come Back to the 5 & Dime, Jimmy Dean, Jimmy Dean*. A member of Circle Rep, Miss Bates has spent several seasons at the O'Neill Playwrights Conference and Robert Redford's Sundance Institute. Her Off-Broadway credits include *Curse of the Starving Class*, the original company of *Vanities* and *The Road to Mecca*. On television she guest starred on *St. Elsewhere, Cagney & Lacey*, the CBS mini-series *Murder Ordained* and the American Playhouse film *One for Sorrow, Two for Joy*. Feature films such as *Straight Time, The Morning After* and *Arthur on the Rocks* have all had the honor of Miss Bates' talents.

ORSON BEAN

Orson Bean was given a magic set at the age of eight, and has never recovered. He developed his illusions into a nightclub act, toured the country as a prestidigitator and made his New York debut as a stand-up comic at the *Blue Angel* supper club. His Broadway appearances include *Almanac*, for which he received a Theatre World Award; the leading role in *Will Success Spoil Rock Hunter*; *Subways are for Sleeping*, for which he received a Tony nomination; and a two-year run in *Never Too Late*. He replaced Anthony Newley in *The Roar of the Greasepaint* and starred opposite Melina Mercouri in *Illya Darling*. Mr. Bean's Off-Broadway production, *Home Movies*, won three Obie Awards. His book, *Me and the Orgone*, was successfully published by St. Martin's Press and is still in print. His recently-authored book, *Too Much is Not Enough,* is due out soon.

DEBRA BIER

Debra Bier has been the assistant to Broadway director/choreographer Arthur Faria for the past eight years. They have created for Broadway musicals, network and PBS television specials, movies and industrial shows. Miss Bier was a founding member of The American Dance Machine and, among other television performances, appeared with Gwen Verdon on *The Dick Cavett Show*. In addition to an extensive performing career, Debra is a renowned teacher of ballet, jazz, tap and aerobics in the U.S., Canada, and throughout Europe and Southeast Asia. She has graced the staff of such prestigious schools as The Harkness Ballet School, The New York School of Dance, The National Dance Institute, Elizabeth Seaton College, Manhattanville and Mercy Colleges and is a member of the Canadian Dance Teachers Association.

DAVID BIRNEY

David Birney graduated with honors from Dartmouth College, was awarded a Dartmouth Fellowship for graduate study, and received an M.A. from the University of California in Los Angeles. Mr. Birney's acting and directing skills have garnered him critical acclaim, important acting challenges, and awards in all theatrical media. He has appeared in numerous films, television features and series which include: *Oh God, Book II*; *Trial by Combat*; *Testimony of Two Men*; *The Adam's Chronicle*; *The Deadly Game,* which was the pilot for his *Serpico* series; *The Bible - Daniel in the Lion's Den; Long Journey Home* and *Bridget Loves Bernie*. Mr. Birney's talents lend themselves to classical and contemporary as well as musical stage roles. From the Young Man in *Summertree,* to Cusins in *Major Barbara,* to Arthur in *Camelot,* and to Salieri in *Amadeus* on Broadway, he has an adaptability not to be equalled. He also appeared on Broadway in *Benefactors,* and directed the Los Angeles premiere of David Mamet's *A Life In The Theatre,* for which he won the *L.A. Weekly* Award for Best Director.

MOM'S CHILI   page 99
IRISH SODA BREAD   page 205

PHILIP BOSCO

Philip Bosco has won three Tony Award nominations for his work in *The Rape of the Belt, You Never Can Tell* and *Heartbreak House*. His other Broadway credits are extensive and illustrious, including performances in *Whose Life is it Anyway?, The Bacchae, Saint Joan, Devil's Disciple* and *Lend Me a Tenor*. Mr. Bosco has a list of film and television credits as impressive as that for the theatre. He appeared in such films as Woody Allen's *Another Woman; Three Men and a Baby; Suspect; Children of a Lesser God; Blue Steel* and *Working Girl*. For the small screen he won an Emmy Award for *Read Between the Lines*, and appeared with Richard Crenna in the miniseries *Internal Affairs*, with Treat Williams in *Echoes in the Dark* and with Frank Langella in *Liberty*.

LOUIS BOTTO

Louis Botto, author of *At This Theatre*, is the Senior Editor of *Playbill*. He is a former Senior Editor of *Look*, where he specialized in theatrical features and a by-line column. His interest in the theatre began in 1937 when he attended his first Broadway show. As a graduate student in speech and theatre at Catholic University, he had a musical and a play produced on campus. The play won a Johns Hopkins Award. Mr. Botto contributed sketches and lyrics to the *New Faces* reviews on Broadway, to Ben Bagley's *Shoestring Review* and Julius Monk's reviews at the Upstairs at the Downstairs Club. He has been guest drama critic on NBC-TV's *Eleven O'Clock News* and has written articles for *The New York Times Magazine*, the *Daily News Magazine*, *The Ladies Home Journal*, *Intellectual Digest* and many other publications. His vast collection of theatrical memorabilia has been exhibited at the Kennedy Center for the Performing Arts.

FETTUCCINE BOTTO   page 112

CAROL BURNETT

Carol Burnett has demonstrated her comic genius, musical abilities and dramatic skill in a varied selection of motion picture, television and theatrical productions. The winner of five Emmy Awards and countless other creative and humanitarian honors, Miss Burnett regularly appeared on *The Garry Moore Show* and starred for eleven years in *The Carol Burnett Show*, the longest running musical-comedy variety program in television history. She starred as Princess Winifred in the Off-Broadway and Broadway productions of *Once Upon a Mattress* and as Hope Springfield in *Fade Out, Fade In*. Carol has starred in two Robert Altman films, *Health* and *A Wedding; The Four Seasons; Annie; Pete and Tillie;* and *The Front Page.* She has had numerous television variety specials: *Julie and Carol at Carnegie Hall, Sills and Burnett at the Met* and *Burnett Discovers Domingo*, in addition to her comic and dramatic performances in *6 Rms Riv Vu, Twigs, Friendly Fire, Life of the Party-The Story of Beatrice, Between Friends,* and *Hostage*, in which she appeared with her daughter Carrie Hamilton. Miss Burnett authored *One More Time*, a book focusing on her life growing up in Hollywood through her initial years in New York. In 1985, Carol was inducted into the television Hall of Fame and was honored with a retrospective tribute at the Museum of Broadcasting in New York.

MADE TO ORDER   page 213

RUTH BUZZI

Ruth Buzzi, whose comic genius has won her the coveted Golden Globe Award, five Emmy Award nominations and the NAACP Image Award, played the Good Fairy in the original Broadway production of *Sweet Charity* with Gwen Verdon. Off-Broadway Miss Buzzi has appeared in *A Man's a Man*, *Little Mary Sunshine*, *Babe's in the Woods*, and *Misguided Tour*. Miss Buzzi's unmatchable talents are probably best remembered from her stint on *Rowan and Martin's Laugh In*; however, she has starred in countless feature films, TV series and specials. Her performances in shows such as *Medical Center*, *Trapper John, M.D.* and the movie of the week *In Name Only* have displayed her versatility and established her as a dramatic actress. With over 80 on-camera TV commercials and 200 voice-over commercials for radio and TV to her credit, Miss Buzzi has been honored as "Best Spokeswoman" by the TV commercial industry twice. Her distinct speaking voice has been heard through many lovable cartoon characters in such films as the Academy Award-winning *The Aristocats* and *It's Tough to be a Bird,* and the series *The Jetsons*, *Marmaduke*, *The Berenstein Bears*, and *Smurfs*, to name a few.

LIZ CALLAWAY

Liz Callaway has been an active performer in the musical theatre since 1979. Most recently she appeard in The Manhattan Theatre Club production of *1-2-3-4-5!* She made her Broadway debut in Stephen Sondheim's *Merrily We Roll Along*, directed by Hal Prince. Miss Callaway's credits include roles both on and Off-Broadway in several musicals, such as *Baby*, for which she was nominated for the Tony Award, *The Three Musketeers* and *The Matinee Kids*. She has also appeared in two specials for PBS: *Follies in Concert* and *In Performance at the White House*. In addition, Liz regularly sings our National Anthem for the World Champion New York Mets. She currently resides in Charlestown, Massachusetts with her husband, Dan Foster, where she hosts a weekday children's program *Ready To Go!* for WNEV-TV.

PASTA CARBONARA   page 118
FUDGE PIE   page 197

NELL CARTER

Nell Carter's rare combination of talent and discipline give her the ability to perform impressive musical, comedy and dramatic roles with equal success. Her dream of "obtaining a secure job in show business" came true with her series *Gimme a Break*. Also for television, Nell appeared in the award-winning *Baryshnikov on Broadway* and as Sgt. Hildy Jones in the weekly series *Lobo*. Two feature films are to her credit: *Hair* and *Back Roads*. It was an appearance on the *Today Show* which brought her national attention and gave her the entree into New York's most popular nightclubs. Broadway welcomed her versatility in *Dude, Don't Bother Me, I Can't Cope, Jesus Christ Superstar, Bury the Dead* and *Ain't Misbehavin'* for which she won unanimous critical acclaim and the Tony Award. Miss Carter recently recreated her *Misbehavin'* role to sold out crowds and rave reviews.

WALTER CHARLES

Walter Charles starred on Broadway in the Tony Award winning musical extravaganza *La Cage aux Folles* in the role of Albin. He also created the role for the highly successful Los Angeles production. Mr. Charles was a member of the Broadway companies of *Cats, Sweeney Todd, Grease, 1600 Pennsylvania Avenue,* and *Knickerbocker Holiday* with Richard Kiley. His beautiful bass-baritone voice has won him numerous singing as well as non-singing roles for stage, television and screen.

COUNTRY CAPTAIN CHICKEN   page 138
MOM'S BREAD PUDDING   page 185

MICHAEL CRAWFORD

Michael Crawford most recently appeared on Broadway as The Phantom in *The Phantom of the Opera*, for which he won the 1988 Tony, Drama Desk, Outer Critics' Circle and Drama League Awards. He also won the Olivier Award for Best Actor in a Musical for the same role in the London production. *Phantom* was his fourth consecutive starring role in a major West End musical following *Barnum* (for which he won his first Olivier Award), *Billy*, and *Flowers for Algernon*. A star of stage, screen and television in London, Mr. Crawford is perhaps best known to American audiences for his co-starring roles in the films *Hello, Dolly!*, *A Funny Thing Happened on the Way to the Forum*, *The Knack*, *The Jokers*, *How I Won the War*, *The Games*, *Hello-Goodbye*, *Alice's Adventures in Wonderland*, and *Condorman*. Born in Salisbury, Wiltshire, he began his professional career as a boy soprano in Benjamin Britten's *Let's Make an Opera*. Numerous TV appearances and over 500 radio broadcasts later found him the popular star of the British television program *Not So Much a Programme, More a Way of Life*, winning the Variety Club Award for Most Promising Actor. Michael has also appeared on the West End in *No Sex Please, We're British* and *Same Time, Next Year*. His first solo album, *The Michael Crawford Album*, recently earned him a platinum record and is available on the Columbia label.

BLYTHE DANNER

Blythe Danner has starred in many distinguished television movies, specials and series, including *F. Scott Fitzgerald and the Last of the Belles, Eccentricities of a Nightingale, A Love Affair: The Eleanor and Lou Gehrig Story, Dr. Cook's Garden,* her own comedy series *Adam's Rib,* and *Tattinger's.* Miss Danner has had notable success on stage and in films. She won the Tony in 1970 for her performance in *Butterflies are Free* and the Theatre World Award for her appearance in *The Miser.* She was also nominated for the Tony for the revival of Tennessee Williams' *A Streetcar Named Desire* and Harold Pinter's *Betrayal.* Some other New York credits include *Blithe Spirit* with Geraldine Page and Richard Chamberlin, and *Much Ado About Nothing* for the New York Shakespeare Festival. Her most recent film role was in Neil Simon's *Brighton Beach Memoirs,* which followed memorable performances in *The Great Santini, Hearts of the West, 1776,* and *Too Far to Go.*

BLYTHE'S CHICKEN   page 135
LENNIE GERSHE'S MYSTERY LUNCH DELIGHT   page 214

RUBY DEE

Ruby Dee is a product of Harlem's American Negro Theatre and the New York City public school system, where she graduated from Hunter College. On stage, Ms. Dee was Lutibelle in her husband Ossie Davis' *Purlie Victorious*, and Ruth in *A Raisin in the Sun*. She won an Obie for her role in *Boesman and Lena* and a Drama Desk Award for *Wedding Band*. She performed Katherine in *The Taming of the Shrew* and Cordelia in *King Lear* for the American Shakespeare Festival, and recently delighted Broadway audiences in *Checkmates* with Denzel Washington. A PBS special, *Martin Luther King: The Dream and the Drum* received critical acclaim, as did her PBS series *With Ossie & Ruby*. In 1983 she received the ACE Award for her portrayal of Mary Tyrone in O'Neill's *Long Day's Journey into Night*. Other TV credits include: *Lincoln, Windmills of the Gods, The Atlanta Child Murders, Roots: The Next Generation, I Know Why the Caged Bird Sings*, and *To Be Young Gifted and Black*. In film, she is perhaps best remembered as Lutibelle in *Gone Are The Days*, as Ruth in *A Raisin In The Sun*, in *Buck and the Preacher*, and as Rachel in *The Jackie Robinson Story*. Ms. Dee is a gifted writer, mother of three grown children and gives concert readings on a variety of themes, as well as special programs from the works of black authors.

JEFFREY DeMUNN

Jeffrey DeMunn received a Tony Award nomination for his performance as Taylor in *K2*. He also starred on Broadway in *Sleight of Hand*, as Horst in *Bent*, Phil in *Comedians,* and opposite Kate Nelligan in *Spoils of War*. He won a Drama Desk Award nomination for his role as Jack in the New York Shakespeare Festival production of *A Prayer for My Daughter*. Mr. DeMunn has appeared in a number of major motion pictures, including *The Blob, Ragtime, The Tender, Betrayed, Warning Sign,* and *Ressurection*. He has created characters in series, episodics and plays for TV on all the major television networks. Some of those credits include: *Windmills of the Gods, Lincoln, Twilight Zone,* and *Mourning Becomes Electra.*

EGYPTIAN BEAN SALAD   page 169
THOMSEN'S FAMOUS MICHIGAN RELISH   page 216

ANDRE DeSHIELDS

Andre DeShields won the coveted Joseph Jefferson Award for his direction of the Chicago premiere of George C. Wolfe's *The Colored Museum* and two Audelco Awards for having directed and choreographed the AMAS Theatre production of *Blackberries*. Mr. DeShields initially achieved national recognition for creating the title role in the Tony Award-winning Broadway musical *The Wiz*. A member of the original company of *Ain't Misbehavin'* at the Manhattan Theatre Club and on Broadway, he won an Emmy Award for recreating his role in the NBC television special of the Fats Waller musical. Other TV credits include the NBC Movie of the Week *I Dream of Jeannie - 15 Years Later*, and two PBS specials, *Alice in Wonderland* and *Ellington: The Music Lives On*. In New York he starred in such shows as *Jazzbo Brown, Just So, L'Histoire du Soldat* at Carnegie Hall, *Stardust, Haarlem Nocturn*, and the revival of *Ain't Misbehavin'*. Recently, Mr. DeShields made his film debut as Sandor in the Empire Pictures release *Prison* and directed Euripedes' *Trojan Women* at the University of Michigan, Ann Arbor.

PHYLLIS DILLER

Phyllis Diller began her show business career at the age of 37. Her raucous laugh and irrepressible humor have made her an international celebrity. She began performing in San Francisco's *Purple Onion* and has performed to capacity crowds in virtually every major supper club in the U.S., Canada, England, Monte Carlo and Australia. Given her fondness for live performing, Miss Diller has quite a list of film and television roles to her credit. She played Texas Guinan in Elia Kazan's *Splendor in the Grass,* and appeared in 12 other films, including Elmer Rice's prize-winning satire *The Adding Machine,* and three films with her friend Bob Hope. An author as well as a poet, she has written four best selling books for Doubleday: *Phyllis Diller's Housekeeping Hints, Phyllis Diller's Marriage Manual, The Complete Mother,* and *The Joys of Aging and How to Avoid Them.* Several comedy albums crystallize the famous Diller wit and image of the housewife's hair-do lament, wacky clothes and lack of housekeeping ability. In private life, Miss Diller is a devoted mother, fine cook, and elegant dresser. Most recently she appeared as Mother Superior in the San Francisco production of *Nunsense.* She considers the highlight of her career her portrayal of Dolly Gallagher Levi in the Broadway production of *Hello, Dolly!*

KENNETH ELLIOTT

Kenneth Elliott began his directorial career with three consecutive Off-Broadway hits: *Times Square Angel, Vampire Lesbians of Sodom,* and *Psycho Beach Party.* All three were written by and starred the comic genius Charles Busch. *Vampires* is currently "the longest-running comedy in New York," now in its fourth year. Mr. Elliott was asked by Joseph Papp to direct the New York Shakespeare Festival production of *Zero Positive,* and is currently developing a musical adaptation of a Joe Orton screenplay, *Up Against It!,* also for Joseph Papp.

ARTHUR FARIA

Arthur Faria was personally selected by Lena Horne to direct and choreograph her triumphant return to Broadway in *Lena Horne: The Lady and Her Music*. This landmark production garnered a Drama Desk Award nomination for Mr. Faria, as well as a special Tony Award for Miss Horne. Mr. Faria is also responsible for the inventive staging and choreography of the Tony Award-winning musical *Ain't Misbehavin'*, which earned him nominations for both the Tony and Drama Desk Awards, and won him an Obie for the original production at the Manhattan Theatre Club. Mr. Faria has staged, choreographed and directed many other successful productions. He has several Off-Broadway hits to his credit, and critics in Washington, D.C. praised his staging and choreography in the highly acclaimed *All Night Strut*. He choreographed for mimes Shields & Yarnell, staged the break-dancing Rock Steady Crew, gave the Village People their bumps and grinds, invented a sophisticated revue for Bobby Short, created a new pas-de-deux for Bolshoi stars Valentina and Leonide Koslov, and directed a Royal Command Performance at the Sinlapakorn National Theatre in Bangkok, Thailand. Among his TV credits are the NBC presentation of *Ain't Misbehavin'*, for which he received an Emmy Award nomination, *Duke Ellington: The Music Lives On* for PBS, and an MTV rock video *Boogie Back to Texas* for Asleep At The Wheel.

CHICKEN ALICE FAYE   page 134
YAM NUA (THAI BEEF SALAD)   page 158

MARGO FEIDEN

Margo Feiden, one of the world's preeminent art dealers for 20 years, is the exclusive representative for master artist Al Hirschfeld and watercolorist Jim McMullan. Both gentlemen are known for their artwork for Broadway shows and of theatre celebrities. The beautiful Margo Feiden Galleries is located in Greenwich Village in New York City. As an author, Miss Feiden has written the definitive book on calories, *The Calorie Factor: The Dieter's Companion*. Miss Feiden is listed in the *Guiness Book of World's Records* as the youngest producer in Broadway history. She was 16 years old when she produced a revival of *Peter Pan*.

VERY SATISFYING BAKED POTATO SKINS   page 176
STUFT SPUDS   page 177

TOVAH FELDSHUH

Tovah Feldshuh received a Tony Award nomination, the Theatre World Award, Obie, Drama Desk and Outer Critics' Circle Awards for her dazzling Broadway performance in *Yentl*. She also received the Outer Critics' Circle Award for *Dreyfus in Rehearsal* and *Rogers and Hart*, and another Tony Award nomination for *Sarava*. Her performance in *The Three Sisters* at the Brooklyn Academy of Music won her a second Drama Desk Award. This award-winning actress is not limited to the stage. Television audiences will recognize Miss Feldshuh from appearances on *Love Boat*, *The Equalizer*, *Bob Newhart*, as Harry Hamlin's ex-wife, Lynn Palmer, on *L.A. Law*, and as Helena Slomova in *The Holocaust*, for which she was nominated for an Emmy Award. She can be seen in the Paramount Pictures release *The Blue Iguana* and in *Cheaper to Keep Her* opposite Mac Davis. Tovah recently starred in the first New York revival of Neil Simon's *The Last of the Red Hot Lovers*, followed by the title role in *Mistress of the Inn* at the Roundabout Theatre, and then back on Broadway in *Lend Me A Tenor* with Philip Bosco.

JOSE FERRER

Jose Ferrer made his Broadway debut in 1935 and won his first Tony Award for his performance in the title role in *Cyrano de Bergerac.* Other memorable Broadway credits include: *The Silver Whistle,* Iago in *Othello,* and his direction and starring as Oscar Jaffe in *Twentieth Century.* He won Tony Awards for his direction of both *The Fourposter* and *Stalag 17.* He produced, directed and appeared in *The Shrike* - the Pulitzer Prize-winning play for which he received three Outer Critics' Circle Awards and two Tonys. He also directed *My Three Angels, The Andersonville Trial, All My Sons* with Lee Richardson for its regional tour, *The Best Man* at the Mark Taper Forum and starred in *The Girl Who Came to Supper* and *Man of La Mancha.* The summer of 1988 was spent in England performing in *Ring Round the Moon* for the Chichester Festival Theatre. Mr. Ferrer has appeared and directed for film, television and opera. He won the Oscar for his signature role of Cyrano de Bergerac and was nominated for *Joan of Arc* and *Moulin Rouge.* Some of his more recent film and television appearances include: *Behind the Iron Mask, To Be Or Not To Be, Dune, Evita, Newhart,* and the PBS production of *Strange Interlude.*

HARVEY FIERSTEIN

Harvey Fierstein is a two-time Tony Award-winning author for *Torch Song Trilogy* and *La Cage aux Folles,* and a Tony Award-winning actor for his brilliantly funny and touching portrayal of Arnold in *Torch Song Trilogy.* His other theatrical efforts include *Safe Sex, Spook House, Forget Him,* and *Legs Diamond* with Peter Allen. This year, Mr. Fierstein made his television acting and writing debut with *Tidy Endings* for HBO, and his film debut with *Torch Song Trilogy - The Movie* for New Line Cinema.

BETTY GARRETT

Betty Garrett is known to TV audiences as Irene Lorenzo, Edith's friend and Archie's nemesis in *All in the Family*, and Edna DeFazio on *Laverne and Shirley*. In movies she was part of the "Golden Era" of the Hollywood musical, appearing in *On The Town*, *Take Me Out to the Ballgame*, *Neptune's Daughter*, *Words and Music*, and *My Sister Eileen*. Miss Garrett's first love, however, has always been the stage. She trained at the Neighborhood Playhouse in New York, where she studied dance with Martha Graham and acting with Sanford Meisner. Her first appearances on the New York stage were with Martha Graham's dance group and with Orson Welles' Mercury Theatre. She went on to understudy Ethel Merman in *Something For the Boys* and on to stardom in *Call Me Mister*, for which she received the Donaldson Award (forerunner to the Tony). Other Broadway shows have been *Laffing Room Only*, *Beg Borrow or Steal*, *A Girl Could Get Lucky*, *Supporting Cast*, and *Spoon River*. *Spoon River* originated in Los Angeles at Theatre West, the 25-year-old workshop of which Betty is one of the founding members. It was there she developed her one woman show *Betty Garrett and Other Songs*, which has played all over the country, winning her the L.A. Drama Critics' Award and The Bay Area Critics Award. She most recently played Mme. Armfeldt in the Theatre West production of *A Little Night Music*.

GARRETT-PARKS LAMB CURRY   page 161
BETTY BEER   page 209

RAY GILL

Ray Gill most recently appeared with Frances Sternhagen in the long running hit *Driving Miss Daisy*, as Miss Daisy's doting son. His Broadway credits are illustrious and include Bruce Granit in *On the Twentieth Century, They're Playing Our Song*, the Pirate King in *Pirates of Penzance, The First* and Stephen Sondheim's *Sunday in the Park with George*. Mr. Gill performed in the workshop productions of *Into The Woods* and Schmidt and Jones' *Grover's Corners* and in *A Bundle of Nerves* at the Top of the Gate.

KIELBASA AND SAUERKRAUT   page 161
THE WORLD'S BEST POTATO SALAD   page 175

ANITA GILLETTE

Anita Gillette received the Drama Critics' Award and a Tony nomination for her performance as Jenny Malone in Neil Simon's *Chapter Two*. She also appeared on Broadway as Blanche in Simon's *Brighton Beach Memoirs*, as Sonja in *They're Playing Our Song, Carnival, Cabaret, Mr. President* and *Don't Drink the Water*. Miss Gillette has appeared at the prestigious Circle Rep in the premiere of Murray Schisgal's *Road Show*, and in John Guare's *Rich and Famous* at Joseph Papp's Public Theatre. She can be seen in the romantic comedy *Moonstruck*, is featured in the CBS television series *Almost Grown*, and has numerous other TV appearances to her credit, such as: *All That Glitters, Marathon, It Happened at Lakewood Manor, Bob & Carol & Ted & Alice*, and a two hour special of *St. Elsewhere*.

DODY GOODMAN

Dody Goodman, star of stage, film and television, began her career as a dancer before gaining a reputation as an extraordinary comedienne. She danced in such Broadway musicals as *High Button Shoes, Call Me Madam, Miss Liberty,* and *Wonderful Town*. It was during *Wonderful Town* that actress Imogene Coca convinced her to put her dancing shoes aside and concentrate on comedy as a career. Ms. Goodman's comedic style has entertained audiences in such Broadway productions as *Period of Adjustment, My Daughter, Your Son, Rainy Day in Newark,* the revival of *The Front Page,* and *Ah, Wilderness!,* for which she received a Drama Desk nomination. To television audiences, Dody was the beloved "Resident Zany" on *Jack Paar's Tonight Show,* and is probably best known for her role as Martha Shumway on the popular series *Mary Hartman, Mary Hartman.* She has appeared as a regular on *Forever Fernwood, Dinah, NBC Bandstand, Girl Talk, Liar's Club, Different Strokes,* and *Punky Brewster,* as well as guest spots on *Murder She Wrote* and *Crazy Like a Fox.* Film credits include *Max Dugan Returns, Grease, Grease II, Splash,* and *Splash II.* Dody is the author of *Mourning in a Funny Hat,* the story of a woman's struggle to develop independence following the death of her husband, and is the author, producer, and star of *Women Women Women,* a comic documentary looking at women's struggle for emancipation.

MORTON GOULD

Morton Gould ranks among the leading citizens of the music world. He has attained world-wide renown as a symphonic composer, conductor, composer of film, television, Broadway and ballet scores, and recording artist. In 1986, Mr. Gould added leadership to his list of achievements when he was elected President of the American Society of Composers, Authors and Publishers. Mr. Gould's many honors include a Grammy Award and twelve Grammy nominations, the 1983 Gold Baton Award, and the 1985 Medal of Honor for Music from the National Arts Club. In 1986, he was elected to the American Academy and Institute of Arts and Letters, and was presented with the National Music Council's Golden Eagle Award. He has composed for symphonies all over the United States, for the Chamber Music Society of Lincoln Center, the New York City Ballet, collaborated with the dance world's most prominent choreographers such as George Balanchine, Elliot Feld, Agnes DeMille and Jerome Robbins. He composed the music for two Broadway musicals: *Arms and the Girl* was the first, and had lyrics by Dorothy Fields. *Billion Dollar Baby*, directed by Jerome Robbins, with lyrics by Comden and Green is currently experiencing a reincarnation in *Jerome Robbins' Broadway*.

PERCIATELLI WITH ANCHOVY/TOMATO SAUCE   page 121

DEBORAH GRAHAM

Deborah Graham, in addition to National Tours of *Jerry's Girls* with Carol Channing, *George M!* with Ken Berry, and *They're Playing Our Song* with Lorna Luft, has appeared on Broadway in *Snoopy, Stardust,* and *Romance, Romance*. Not only is she an accomplished singer and dancer, but a pianist as well. Her talents have also earned her appearances on the daytime dramas *The Guiding Light* and *The Edge of Night*.

JOEL GREY

Joel Grey has been performing since the age of nine. His rich and varied career encompasses every medium of the entertainment industry. Mr. Grey is probably best known for his performance as the M.C. in *Cabaret*. His acclaimed Broadway performance won him the Tony Award and the recreation of the role for the film version, with Liza Minnelli, won him the Oscar. Some of his other Broadway credits include: *Come Blow Your Horn*, *Half a Sixpence*, *Stop the World I Want to Get Off*, and Tony nominations for *George M!*, *Goodtime Charlie*, and *The Grand Tour*. In addition to the Tony and the Oscar, Mr. Grey has been the recipient of many other awards in the entertainment field. He has been named Entertainer of the Year by the American Guild of Variety Artists, received the Drama Desk, Outer Critics' Circle, Variety Critics' Award twice, the Golden Globe and was recently honored with a star bearing his name on the Hollywood Walk of Fame. The string of shows, motion pictures, television and nightclub appearances has not stopped since Mr. Grey was first spotted in his father's (the late comedian Mickey Katz) stage revue by Eddie Cantor and presented on the *Colgate Comedy Hour*. Recently, he restaged the national tour of *Zorba* with Anthony Quinn, starred in the Public Theatre production of *The Normal Heart*, and was requested to perform at the White House for West German Chancellor Helmut Schmidt, and again for Chancelor Helmut Kohl, President and Mrs. Reagan.

JOEL GREY'S RISO ALFREDO   page 122

UTA HAGEN

Uta Hagen made her professional debut at 18 as Ophelia in Eva LeGallienne's production of *Hamlet* and her Broadway debut, the same year, as Nina in the Lunts' famous production of *The Seagull*. She appeared on Broadway opposite Paul Muni in *Key Largo*, as Desdemona in *Othello*, in the revival of *Angel Street* and as Blanche DuBois in *A Streetcar Named Desire*. In 1950, she won her first Tony Award for *The Country Girl*. She also starred on Broadway in Shaw's *Saint Joan*, the revival of *Tovarich*, *In Any Language*, *The Magic and The Loss*, *The Island of Goats*, *A Month in the Country*, and in Brecht's *The Good Woman of Sezuan*. In 1962, she created the role of Martha in *Who's Afraid of Virginia Woolf?*, for which she received her second Tony and The Drama Desk Award. Miss Hagen repeated the role in the London production and won The London Critics' Award. Miss Hagen returned to the Broadway stage in *Charlotte*, and appeared in *You Never Can Tell* at Circle in the Square. Miss Hagen is the author of *Respect for Acting*, *Love for Cooking*, and a memoir, *Success*. She has three honorary doctorates, received the Mayor's Liberty Medal in 1986, the John Houseman Award in 1987, and was inducted into the Theatre Hall of Fame in 1981. Since the Fall of 1947, Miss Hagen has been on the faculty of The H.B. Studio, where she has trained many of the outstanding actors of the American Stage and Screen.

HELEN HAYES

Helen Hayes is the first lady of the American theatre.

HELEN HAYES' CURRY MOUSSE   page 101

AL HIRSCHFELD

Al Hirschfeld has been creating his signature line drawings of Broadway cast members for the *New York Times* almost every Sunday (and every Friday since 1976) since the early 1920's. The list of theatre dignitaries who have been honored with a Hirschfeld rendering is awe-inspiring. It is considered by some that to be drawn by Hirschfeld is to have "arrived." It all began when Mr. Hirschfeld and a friend, publicist Richard Maney, were attending a Broadway play. During the performance, Hirschfeld scribbled a sketch of the leading actor, Sacha Guitry, on his program. Maney grabbed it, asked Hirschfeld to transfer it to a clean piece of paper, and it was quickly sold to *The New York Herald Tribune* and a regular feature in *The New York Times* began soon after. In 1945, Dolly Haas Hirschfeld gave birth to a beautiful little girl named Nina, and since that day the proud father has been playing a game with his viewers. In each drawing is hidden his daughter's name. The number of "Ninas" written next to the artists signature denotes the number of times the name will appear. If there is no number, it is understood that one "Nina" appears. Mr. Hirschfeld's portraits are on display at the Margo Feiden Galleries in New York.

NASI GORING   page 142

ROBERT HOSHOUR

Robert Hoshour's acrobatic skills and deftness on the flying trapeze won him a place in the company of *Barnum* on Broadway. He then went on to appear in *The Little Prince and the Aviator* with Michael York, the original cast of *Cats* as Tumblebrutus and, most recently, *Romance, Romance*. Mr. Hoshour's talents are not only musical. He has performed nationally as Ariel in *The Tempest* and Cassio in *Othello*.

SPINACH TOFU LASAGNE   page 172
MORNING TOFU PIE   page 200

KIM HUNTER

Kim Hunter made her Broadway debut as Stella in *A Streetcar Named Desire* in December 1947, for which she won both the Donaldson and Critics' Awards. She later won an Academy Award, Look Magazine Award, and The Hollywood Foreign Correspondents' Golden Globe for her performance in the film version of the play. In addition to *Streetcar*, some of her films include *Stairway to Heaven, Deadline: USA, Lilith, The Kindred,* and the first three of the highly successful *Planet of the Apes* quintet, in which she played the chimpanzee psychiatrist, Dr. Zira. Her numerous stage appearances include starring roles in *Darkness at Noon, The Children's Hour, The Tender Trap, Write Me a Murder, Weekend,* the revival of *The Women,* and *To Grandmother's House We Go* - all on Broadway. Miss Hunter has made hundreds of television and regional stage appearances, and is the author of an autobiographical cookbook entitled *Loose in the Kitchen.*

JEREMY IRONS

Jeremy Irons made his motion picture debut in Herbert Ross' *Nijinski*. His next film role was as the man who became obsessed by Meryl Streep in *The French Lieutenant's Woman*, which won him the Variety Club Award for Best Actor and a British Academy Award nomination. This was followed by his acclaimed performances in the award-winning *Moonlighting* and Harold Pinter's *Betrayal*. His first London stage appearance was opposite David Essex in *Godspell*, which led to his work with The Young Vic and the New Shakespeare Company. He appeared in the West End in *Wild Oats* and *The Rear Column,* for which he won the Clarence Derwent Award. In 1983, he appeared on Broadway in Tom Stoppard's *The Real Thing* and won both the Drama League and Tony Awards for Best Actor. This award-winning performer has also starred in many television series. He is best known for his portrayal of Charles Ryder in *Brideshead Revisited,* which brought him world-wide acclaim and nominations for the Emmy, British Academy and Golden Globe Awards. His major motion picture performances include: *Swann in Love; The Mission* with Robert DeNiro; as twin gynecologists in *Dead Ringers*; in Alan Ayckbourn's comedy *A Chorus of Disapproval; Danny, the Champion of the World;* and *Australia.*

ELAINE JOYCE

Elaine Joyce created the title role in the original company of *Sugar* on Broadway and starred in *An Evening With Jule Styne* at the legendary Rainbow Room. Miss Joyce, in addition to numerous appearances in plays and musicals across the country, has sung and danced her way in some of the most famous movie musicals of all time including *Funny Girl* and *Bye Bye Birdie*. She has guest starred on dozens of dramatic series and specials for television. Some of her most recent include: *Simon and Simon, Magnum P.I., Murder, She Wrote,* and *The Bob Hope Special*.

MATZO BREI   page 214

NICK KALEDIN

Nick Kaledin is an M.F.A. graduate of the American Conservatory Theatre in California. There he appeared in numerous productions, such as: *Mourning Becomes Electra, Much Ado About Nothing* and *Hay Fever*. Mr. Kaledin played Foster in *The Octette Bridge Club* on Broadway, directed by Tom Moore. Some of his Off-Broadway credits include *Becoming Memories, Black Coffee, Oliver Oliver* and the smash-hit comedy *Vampire Lesbians of Sodom*, where he played the dashing King Carlisle.

JEAN LeCLERC

Jean LeClerc is best known for his portrayal of Jeremy Hunter on ABC's *All My Children*. After leaving his pre-med studies behind, Jean toured both the U.S. and Canada in theatrical productions and was twice awarded the Fleur De Lys Award. It was his co-starring role opposite Zoe Caldwell in *Divine Sarah*, a drama on the life of Sarah Bernhardt, that lead to his starring role on Broadway as *Dracula*. He enjoyed a successful two year run in the role and since then has gained an impressive list of theatrical and television credits. He has apppeared in the series *T.J. Hooker, The Greatest American Hero* and *The Devlin Connection*. Mr. LeClerc spends much of his free time fund raising for the Cystic Fibrosis Foundation, the Make A Wish Foundation and the American Cancer Society.

MICHELE LEE

Michele Lee, who stars as Karen Fairgate MacKenzie on the top-rated dramatic series *Knots Landing*, got her beginnings on Broadway from her first professional audition. A musical review called *Vintage 60*, set to play Hollywood, was casting just as Michele was graduating from high school. Her parents reluctantly allowed her to audition, she got the part, stopped the show with the number "Five Piece Band and a Woman Who Sings the Blues," and was taken to Broadway by David Merrick to continue in the New York production. After the show closed, she returned to L.A. to star in two more reviews but soon got wind of a new Broadway musical called *Bravo Giovanni*. With borrowed air fare, Miss Lee flew to New York and got the part of a young Italian-American girl who visits Italy and falls for an older man. *Bravo* ran three months and, before it closed, Michele was signed to star opposite Robert Morse in *How to Succeed in Business Without Really Trying*. She played the role of Rosemary for over two years and made her screen debut in the film version. Miss Lee also appeared on Broadway in *Seesaw*. She won rave reviews, not to mention the Drama Desk Award, the Outer Critics' Circle Award and a Tony Award Nomination.

COFFEE CAKE WITH QUICK MIX METHOD   page 190

HAL LINDEN

Hal Linden has earned two Emmy Awards and the Tony. This versatile performer began his show business career, not as the actor/singer he is known to be, but as a clarinet player. Later he toured as a singer with the Sammy Kaye, Bobby Sherwood and Boyd Raeburn bands. After his discharge from the Army, where his interest in acting was piqued by performing in Army revues, Mr. Linden began to study acting and got his first break in 1958. He was signed to understudy Sydney Chaplin in *Bells are Ringing*. Five days later, he was signed to replace Chaplin and starred opposite Judy Holliday both on Broadway and in the national tour. His list of hit Broadway shows has built steadily since. He starred in *On a Clear Day You Can See Forever*, *Subways are for Sleeping*, *The Apple Tree*, *Illya Darling*, *Wildcat*, the revival of *Pajama Game*, *Three Men on a Horse*, *The Rothschilds*, which won him the Tony and, most recently, *I'm Not Rappaport*. His television series, specials, and films include: *Barnie Miller*; *Blacke's Magic*; *FYI*; *Animals, Animals, Animals* (a Peabody Award winner); *Hal Linden's Big Apple*; *My Wicked, Wicked Ways*; and *When You Coming Back, Red Ryder?*, and have all won critical acclaim and great popular success. Mr. Linden has served as national chairman of The March of Dimes and has helped raise some 75 million dollars as host of their annual telethon.

CHEESE-MUSTARD LOAF   page 204

JACKIE MASON

Jackie Mason, one of the best known figures from the golden age of television comedians, has been hailed for his comic genius and versatility. His one-man Broadway show, *The World According to Me!*, won The Tony Award. His Warner Brothers comedy album, based on the show, was nominated for a Grammy and his television special of the same name was nominated for an Emmy Award. Mr. Mason is the author of two books. One is based on his smash hit Broadway show and the other is an hilarious and moving autobiography entitled *Jackie, OY!* Born in Sheboygan, Wisconsin and raised on the Lower East Side of Manhattan, Mr. Mason grew up surrounded by rabbis. His three brothers, his father, his grandfather, his great grandfather were all rabbis, as were his great, great grandfather and his great, great, great.... It comes as no surprise that Jackie was a canter until the age of 25, when he was ordained a rabbi. Three years later he quit the synagogue to become a comedian because, as he says, "Someone in the family had to make a living."

JACKIE MASON'S PERFECT EGG CREAM   page 210

WALTER MATTHAU

Walter Matthau has starred in dozens of unforgettable major motion pictures throughout his long and impressive career. *Face in the Crowd, Slaughter on Tenth Avenue, Goodbye Charlie, The Odd Couple, Cactus Flower, Hello, Dolly!, Plaza Suite, The Front Page, I Ought to be in Pictures, The Bad News Bears,* and *The Couch Trip* are but a few. In 1966, he won the Academy Award as Best Supporting Actor for *The Fortune Cookie* and was nominated twice in the Best Actor category for *Kotch* and *The Sunshine Boys.* Mr. Matthau was the winner of the Tony Award in 1962 for *A Shot in the Dark* and again in 1965 for *The Odd Couple.*

KASHA PORK CASSEROLE   page 160

RUE McCLANAHAN

Rue McClanahan is an award winning actress of the stage and television. Her performance in *Who's Happy Now?* earned her an Obie Award and lead to a multitude of stage roles including the Broadway productions of *Jimmy Shine*, *Sticks and Bones*, and *California Suite*. Ms. McClanahan received the 1987 Emmy Award for Best Actress with her portrayal of the devilish Blanche in the hit comedy series *Golden Girls*, in which she stars. She has also co-starred on *Mama's Family* and *Maude*; made guest appearances on *Trapper John, M.D.*, *Crazy Like a Fox*, *Murder, She Wrote* and *Bob Newhart*; and had a series of her own called *Apple Pie*. For PBS, Ms. McClanahan has been featured in the television versions of the plays: *Hogan's Goat*, *The Rimers of Eldritch*, *Who's Happy Now?*, and *The Skin of Our Teeth*. Some of her movies made for television include: *Word of Honor*, *Topper*, *Take My Daughters, Please*, *The Man in the Brown Suit*, and *Liberace*. A number of feature films are also to her credit, such as: *They Might Be Giants* with George C. Scott, *The People Next Door* with Eli Wallach, and *The Pursuit of Happiness*.

MAUREEN McGOVERN

Maureen McGovern is the most versatile singer of our time. She is an interpreter of jazz, a concert soprano, scat singer par excellence, delineator of the classics, and powerful in her theatrical performances of Broadway show tunes. Ms. McGovern developed her skillful ear at an early age by taking turns singing along with each member of her father's barber shop quartet. That early interest in music has turned into a career of diverse musical successes. Her first No. 1 single, the Acadamy Award-winning *The Morning After*, was followed a few years later by the hits: *Can You Read My Mind,* which also reached No. 1, and *Different Worlds* (the theme from the TV series *Angie)*. Ms. McGovern has toured the country in productions of *The Sound of Music, South Pacific, Guys and Dolls* and *I Do!, I Do!,* and appeared on Broadway in *The Pirates of Penzance* and starred opposite Raul Julia in *Nine*. She has sung in the most impressive concert halls and night clubs in the world and with some of the country's finest symphonies. Her two current albums, *Another Woman in Love* and *State of the Heart*, have been critically acclaimed and will be followed by *Naughty Baby*, a selection of her personal Gershwin favorites taped before a live audience.

JOHN McMARTIN

John McMartin's stage, screen and television credits go on and on. From the TV miniseries *Lincoln* to an episode of *The Golden Girls*, from the fine feature film *All the Presidents Men* to *Pennies From Heaven*, Mr. McMartin's talents adapt and shine in any medium. On Broadway he won a Tony Award nomination for his performance in *Sweet Charity*, and not only a Tony nomination but also a Drama Desk Award for his role in *Don Juan*. He graced the Broadway stage in *Solomon's Child*, *Happy New Year*, *Follies*, and *The Great God Brown*, just to name a few. He has performed at Joseph Papp's Public Theatre in *The Misanthrope* and, as Caesar, in *Julius Caesar* with Al Pacino, Martin Sheen and Ed Herrmann.

FRESH EGG NOODLES
(for a big pot of chicken soup)   page 104

SYLVIA MILES

Sylvia Miles is a two-time Academy Award nominee for *Midnight Cowboy* and *Farewell My Lovely*. Miss Miles is a celebrated stage actress having been nominated Actress of the Year in Great Britain for Tennessee Williams' *Vieux Carre* in 1978. Her numerous stage roles include: *Night of the Iguana* with Richard Chamberlain, *The Iceman Cometh* and *The Balcony*, all at Circle in the Square. Miss Miles starred this past season in *Tea With Mommy and Jack* at the Hudson Guild Theatre in New York, and can be seen in three recent major motion pictures: *Wall Street, Crossing Delancy* and *Spike of Bensonhurst*. Miss Miles is also a rated chess player excelling in rapid transit chess tournaments.

MY FAST CHICKEN   page 139
HAMBURGER CURRY a la SYLVIA MILES   page 152

JAN MINER

Jan Miner holds the honor of being the longest running character in TV advertising: Palmolive Dishwashing Liquid's Madge the Manicurist. Besides portraying Madge, Miss Miner is one of America's busiest and most versatile performers. She no sooner completes one demanding role than she is on to another. On Broadway she has appeared as the aristocratic Fanny Farrell in *Watch on the Rhine,* as the nurse in *Romeo and Juliet* directed by Ted Mann, the comic Cockney nurse in Shaw's *Heartbreak House,* in *Saturday Sunday Monday, The Heiress, The Women,* and *Othello.* Her television and film credits are equally diverse and impressive. She received an Emmy Award for her performance in *Gertrude Stein and a Companion,* appeared on *Cagney and Lacey, One Day at a Time,* and *The Jackie Gleason Show.* She appeared in the films: *Willie and Phil, Endless Love,* and played Lenny Bruce's raucous mother in *Lenny.*

LIZA MINNELLI

Liza Minnelli has won three Tony Awards for her performances in *Flora, the Red Menace, Liza at the Winter Garden*, and *The Act*, and was nominated a fourth time for *The Rink*. Miss Minnelli has received numerous distinctions in her career. She was the youngest actress to receive the Tony (in 1965, at the age of 19), she broke all box office records for her one-woman show at the Winter Garden, and was the first performer to sell out Carnegie Hall for a full week. She has also been the recipient of the Oscar for her dazzling performance in *Cabaret*, not to mention the Golden Globe, British Academy and David di Donatello Awards; an Oscar nomination for *The Sterile Cuckoo*; an Emmy Award for her television special *Liza With a Z* and a second Golden Globe for her starring role in the made for television movie *A Time to Live*. Miss Minnelli's many other film, stage and television appearances have won her kudos from critics and peers alike. Some other credits include the films: *Tell Me That You Love Me, Junie Moon; Lucky Lady; New York, New York; Rent a Cop; Arthur* and *Arthur on the Rocks*. The TV specials include: *Liza; Goldie and Liza Together;* and *Best Foot Forward*. Some of her recordings are: *Liza With a Z; Liza Minnelli: The Singer; Liza Minnelli: Live at the Winter Garden; Tropical Nights; The Act; The Rink* and *Live at Carnegie Hall*.

MARCIA MITZMAN

Marcia Mitzman has appeared on Broadway as Svetlana in *Chess*, the widow in *Zorba* with Anthony Quinn, Rizzo in *Grease* and in the revival of *Oliver!* with Ron Moody. Miss Mitzman starred as Mrs. Lovett in the Lincoln Center revival of *Sweeny Todd* directed by Harold Prince and in two New York City Opera productions: as Nellie in *South Pacific* and Meg in *Brigadoon*. Marcia was born in Manhattan and raised in Hastings-on-Hudson; studied theatre at The High School of Performing Arts, S.U.N.Y at Purchase and at the Neighborhood Playhouse.

ROBERT MORSE

Robert Morse won both the Tony and Drama Desk Awards for his performance in *How to Succeed in Business Without Really Trying*. He earned another Tony nomination when he created the role of Jerry/Daphne in David Merrick's *Sugar,* which was adapted from the film *Some Like it Hot*. Also on Broadway, Mr. Morse appeared with Ruth Gordon in *The Matchmaker,* Jackie Gleason and Walter Pidgeon in *Take Me Along,* in *Say, Darling* and *So Long 174th Street*. Aside from many television appearances, his credits include the motion picture version of *How to Succeed...,* as well as *Guide for the Married Man* and the Hans Christian Anderson fable *The Emperors New Clothes,* in which he co-stars with Sid Caesar. Recently, Mr. Morse appeared as Sidney Black in Moss Hart's *Light Up the Sky* at the London Old Vic and the Ahmanson Theatre in L.A., followed by his portrayal of Scooter Malloy in the musical *Mike* based on the life of Mike Todd, performed at the Walnut Street Theatre in Philadelphia.

YANKEE MEATLOAF   page 153
MAPLE-RASPBERRY CUSTARD   page 187

BEBE NEUWIRTH

Bebe Neuwirth last appeared on Broadway as Nickie in *Sweet Charity* for which she won a Drama Desk nomination and a Tony Award. Her other Broadway performances include Shiela in *A Chorus Line*, Monique in *Little Me* and as a principle dancer in Bob Fosse's *Dancin'*. Miss Neuwirth also appeared in several pre-Broadway workshops including *Kicks* by Tom Eyon and Alan Minken and *13 Days to Broadway* by Cy Coleman, Barbara Fried and Russel Baker. At Upstairs at O'Neils she played eleven different characters in Martin Charnin's comedy review and recently she played Anita in *West Side Story* at the Cleveland Opera. On television, Bebe can be seen as Dr. Lilith Sternin, M.D., PhD., EdD., APA on *Cheers*.

PHYLLIS NEWMAN

Phyllis Newman has been making audiences laugh - on Broadway, in films and on television - for over 25 years. Phyllis got a taste of the theatre life when she appeared, at an early age, as "Baby Phyllis" and sang Carmen Miranda songs between showings at vaudeville theatres in Atlantic City. Several years later her show business career began in earnest when she moved to New York and landed the part of Judy Holliday's standby in *Bells are Ringing*. Shortly after marrying playwright/lyricist Adolph Green, Miss Newman triumphed on Broadway in *Subways are for Sleeping* and went on to win the Tony as Best Featured Actress for her performance. She also starred on Broadway in *The Prisoner of Second Avenue*, *Wish You Were Here*, *Pleasures and Palaces*, *The Apple Tree*, the revival of *On the Town*, *Moonbirds*, her one woman show *The Madwoman of Central Park West*, the concert version of Stephen Sondheim's *Follies*, and *Broadway Bound*, for which she was nominated for a second Tony Award. She appeared on television in NBC's satirical *This is the Week That Was*, as guest host of *The Tonight Show*, *Broadway Sings: The Music of Julie Styne*, *The Equalizer* and *One Life to Live*. Miss Newman recently added "author" to her list of accomplishments when her autobiography entitled *Just in Time* was published by Simon & Schuster. The book traces her childhood, marriage, early success on Broadway, and battle with breast cancer; all with honesty and humor.

KEN PAGE

Ken Page received the 1978 Drama Desk Award as Best Actor in a Musical for his performance in the original Broadway cast of *Ain't Misbehavin'*. Mr. Page was also with the Off-Broadway, L.A., NBC-TV and Paris companies of the Fats Waller musical. In 1976, he made his Broadway debut in the black revival of *Guys and Dolls*, winning the coveted Theatre World Award. The following year he joined the cast of *The Wiz* as the Cowardly Lion. 1982 brought the role of Old Deuteronomy in the original Broadway cast of *Cats*. Mr. Page conceived, wrote the book and directed two L.A. workshop productions of the musical *To Sir With Love*, based on the classic novel and subsequent film. *Sir* and his new musical, *Bebop*, are scheduled for New York productions. Ken has performed his highly acclaimed concert/club act in Caesars Atlantic City, Los Angeles' Universal Ampitheatre and numerous New York nightspots. He starred in *Duke Ellington: The Music Lives On* for PBS, *Broadway Plays Washington* from the Kennedy Center and *To Basie With Love* from Radio City Music Hall. He has guest starred on *Gimme a Break, Scarecrow and Mrs. King*, the pilot for *The Equalizer* and the ABC series *Sable*. He can be heard as the voice of King Gator on the soundtrack of the new animated feature *All Dogs Go to Heaven*. Mr. Page can be seen in the film version of Harvey Fierstein's wonderful Broadway play *Torch Song Trilogy*.

HOWARD PERLOFF

Howard Perloff is a graduate of The Juilliard School of Music. A man of diverse theatrical interests, Mr. Perloff began his association with the theatre as a stage manager for numerous Broadway musicals, the first being *A Joyful Noise* starring John Raitt. He was owner and producer of Long Island's first dinner theatre, The Southampton Cabaret Theatre, which employed many of Broadway's finest performers, such as Chita Rivera in *Irma La Douce*. He went on to work as associate producer for the Broadway production of *Torch Song Trilogy* and as co-producer of the recent *Legs Diamond*. He is also the leader of a highly successful orchestra, based with The Entertainment Group, Inc. of Philadelphia.

TOMMY RALL

Tommy Rall was born in Kansas City, Missouri, raised in Seattle, and first appeared on the vaudeville stage at the age of eight. His first New York appearance came at the Metropolitan Opera House, where he was a principal dancer with the American Ballet Theatre for five seasons. His first Broadway show was *Look, Ma, I'm Dancin'!* followed by *Small Wonder, Miss Liberty, Call Me Madam* and *Juno,* for which he received The Outer Critics' Circle Award. Then he co-starred in *Milk and Honey, Cafe Crown* and *Cry For Us All.* In Hollywood, he had featured roles in many films including *Seven Brides for Seven Brothers, Kiss Me Kate, My Sister Eileen, Pennies From Heaven,* and *Dancers.*

LEE ROY REAMS

Lee Roy Reams received both a Tony and a Drama Desk nomination for his starring performance in 42nd Street - one of the longest running musicals in Broadway history. In his first Broadway role, Mr. Reams won rave reviews as Duane Fox, Lauren Bacall's confidant, in the musical *Applause*. He continued on Broadway with Carol Channing in *Lorelei* and *Hello, Dolly!* Richard Rogers personally selected him to play Will Parker in his production of *Oklahoma* at Lincoln Center. Lee Roy's numerous TV appearances include *In Performance at the White House* for President and Mrs. Reagan, Alexander Cohn's *Happy Birthday Hollywood*, *Night of 100 Stars*, The 1985 and 1986 *Tony Awards Shows* and *The Tonight Show*. He has sung with the Cincinnati Symphony Orchestra, the Illinois Philharmonic and in Venice at Teatro La Fenice in *A Tribute to Leonard Bernstein*.

ALYSON REED

Alyson Reed, who was featured as Cassie in the film version of *A Chorus Line*, starred in the Broadway revival of *Cabaret*, for which received a Tony Award nomination. She appeared in *Dancin', Oh Brother, Dance a Little Closer,* and *Gotta Get Away* - all on Broadway. Her performance in *Marilyn: An American Fable* won her critical acclaim. Off-Broadway, Miss Reed played Audrey in *Little Shop of Horrors* and Karen in the concertized version of *Jubilee* at Town Hall.

ANN REINKING

Ann Reinking is Broadway's top triple threat. Her singing, dancing and acting talents have won her the Theatre World, Outer Critics' Circle, and Clarence Derwent Awards. Miss Reinking received a Tony Award nomination for her performance in Bob Fosse's *Dancin'* and a Tony nomination and Drama Desk nomination as Best Actress for *Good Time Charlie*. Her other Broadway credits include *Cabaret*, *Pippin*, *Over Here*, *A Chorus Line*, *Chicago* and *Sweet Charity*. She has starred in several motion pictures, among them: *Movie Movie* with George C. Scott, *All That Jazz*, *Annie* and *Mickie and Maude*. She has danced at the prestigious Spoleto Festival in Italy with Gary Chryst and in *La Davina* for RAI Television in Pisa, Italy with Mark Silver of the Royal Ballet. Her numerous American television appearances include *Gala of Stars* with Anthony Dowell and *An Invitation to the Dance* with Julie Andrews and Rudolf Nureyev. Most recently, Miss Reinking won the Jefferson Award as Best Choreographer for her choreography in *Pal Joey* at the Goodman Theatre.

DEBBIE REYNOLDS

Debbie Reynolds got her start in show business at the age of sixteen when she entered a local California beauty contest. She didn't think she would win, but she did want the free silk blouse and scarf that were given to each contestant. She did win, however, and along with the title of Miss Burbank came a screen test. She was given a few small parts before her career was launched with a featured role in the classic film *Singin' in the Rain* with Gene Kelly. Many hit movies followed including *I Love Melvin, How the West Was Won, Tammy and the Bachelor, Mary, Mary, The Unsinkable Molly Brown* for which she won an Oscar nomination, *The Singing Nun,* and *Divorce American Style,* to name a few. When movie roles were scarce, Miss Reynolds extended her career into nightclubs, television, and theatre. Her Broadway debut in the title role of *Irene* was a triumph and won her a Tony nomination. Debbie Reynolds is the author of *Debbie: My Life,* and has created a best-selling exercise video, *Do It Debbie's Way.*

JOAN RIVERS

Joan Rivers is an award-winning comedienne, author, actress, writer, director, nightclub headliner, TV talk show hostess and mother to her daughter Melissa. She began her career entertaining in tiny clubs, then moved on to Greenwich Village cabarets and, later, honed her skills at Chicago's *Second City*. Today, Miss Rivers performs in the finest showrooms across the country. Joan produced a syndicated column for the *Chicago Tribune*; authored three books: *Having a Baby Can be a Scream*, *The Life and Times of Heidi Abromowitz* and *Enter Talking*. After writing for *Candid Camera* and writing and starring in *That Show*, she wrote the critically acclaimed *The Girl Most Likely To* for ABC-TV. In addition to her post as permanent guest host on *The Tonight Show* and hosting *The Late Show With Joan Rivers*, Joan caused a sensation with her one-hour comedy special *Joan Rivers and Friends Salute Heidi Abromowitz*. Her comedy album, *What Becomes a Semi-Legend Most?* was nominated for a Grammy. She made her directorial debut with the comedy film *Rabbit Test*, and her Broadway debut in *Fun City*. She returned to Broadway in 1988 in Neil Simon's *Broadway Bound*. Miss Rivers' signature question, "Can We Talk?," has reached such major proportions that the U.S. government has officially registered it as a federal trademark. Her charity efforts have gotten her named national chairperson of the Cystic Fibrosis Foundation, and the Humanitarian of the Year for her frontier fundraising efforts in the fight against AIDS.

JOAN RIVERS' TOAST   page 217

DAVID ROMANO

David Romano is a versatile young tenor who moves with equal ease from musical theatre to grand opera. He recently recorded the soundtrack and was featured in the ABC movie of the week *Infidelity*. He sang a duet with Pavarotti in MGM's *Yes, Georgio* and has performed in over 100 concerts as soloist with Roger Wagner. He has appeared with the S.F. Opera, Opera Colorado, the Ojai Festival and many orchestras on the West Coast. Theatre credits include *Evita*, *Sammy Cahn's Words and Music, Camelot, Kismet* and *The Phantom of the Opera* on Broadway. Some of his other television and film credits are *Fernwood 2 Nite*, *Twilight Zone, Alf, Lady Blue* and *Means and Ends*.

FRANCESCO SCAVULLO

Francesco Scavullo has photographed countless celebrities for every major magazine in the world. He has created dozens of record album covers and his movie posters of *The Main Event* and *A Star is Born* have become collector's items. For Broadway, Mr. Scavullo has shot a wide variety of actors and actresses. His photograph of Raquel Welch was used as the poster for *Woman of the Year,* and his shot of Raul Julia and Anita Morris in *Nine* was made into a giant billboard that towered over Times Square. Mr. Scavullo also photographs commissioned portraits and recently extended his expertise into the art world by creating silk-screened portraits and still lifes which are represented by many fine galleries around the world. Mr. Scavullo is the author of four books: *Scavullo On Beauty, Scavullo Men, Scavullo Women*, and a retrospective, *Scavullo.*

STEAM-BROILED FISH   page 128
STEAMED HERBED VEGETABLES   page 180

HARVEY SCHMIDT

Harvey Schmidt composed music to the words of his partner Tom Jones for a summer production of *The Fantasticks* at Barnard College in 1959. Since its Off-Broadway opening at the Sullivan Street Playhouse in May 1960, it has gone on to become the world's longest running musical and the longest running show in the history of the American theatre. On Broadway, the team has been represented by *110 in the Shade, I Do! I Do!* with Mary Martin and Robert Preston, and by the original musical *Celebration*. For several years they worked privately at Portfolio, their own theatre workshop in New York. The most notable of these efforts was *Philemon*, an original musical which won the Outer Critics' Circle Award in 1975. *Grover's Corners*, their new musical based on Thorton Wilder's classic play *Our Town*, is now in preparation for a U.S. tour. Mr. Schmidt has also won numerous New York Art Director's Club Awards and Society of Illustrators Awards for his work as a painter and graphic artist.

DEBBIE SHAPIRO

Debbie Shapiro is the brassy voiced beauty of many Broadway shows and New York nightclub appearances. She is currently bringing the house down in *Jerome Robbins' Broadway* with her rendition of "Mr. Monotony" by Irving Berlin and as the horn blowing Mazeppa in a scene from *Gypsy*. She also appeared on Broadway in *Blues in the Night*, *Zorba* with Anthony Quinn, the original cast of *They're Playing Our Song*, and received a Drama Desk nomination for her performance in *Perfectly Frank*.

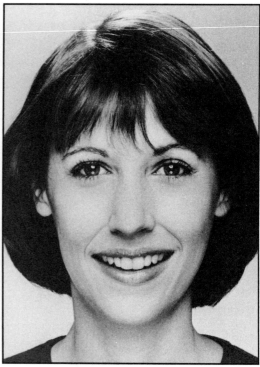

JOHN SIMON   PATRICIA HOAG

John Simon and Patricia Hoag are a well known "Theatre Couple."

Mr. Simon was born in Yugoslavia and studied there, in England and in The United States. He holds a doctorate in comparative literature from Harvard. He has taught at several colleges and universities, written and edited over a dozen books and received three awards in criticism: the George Jean Nathan Award for drama, the George Polk Award for film and the American Academy of Arts & Letters Award for literature. Mr. Simon is currently the drama critic for *New York Magazine*, film critic for *The National Review* and culture critic for *The New Leader*.

Miss Hoag, a graduate of Florida Atlantic University with an M.F.A. in acting and directing, attended Baldwin College and the Boston Conservatory of Music. For two years she was the casting director for the reputable WPA Theatre and is currently working as a theatrical agent placing some of Broadway's most notable celebrities.

BEEF CURRY   page 151
SACHER TORTE   page 201

REX SMITH

Rex Smith signed a recording contract with Columbia Records at age 20 and has recorded six albums to date. While waiting for his album *Sooner or Later* to be released, which went platinum in 1979, he auditioned for a part in the Broadway musical *Grease* and was soon making his Broadway debut as Danny Zuko. That success was followed by the role of Frederic, for which he received a Tony nomination, in Joseph Papps' Shakespeare Festival production of *The Pirates of Penzance*. The show played Broadway, toured for more than two years and was made into a feature film in 1982. He also appeared on Broadway in *The Human Comedy*, starred in the Off-Broadway musical *Brownstone* and played Tony in the Kennedy Center's *West Side Story*, which was the first revival sanctioned by Leonard Bernstein. For television, he starred in the NBC movie *Sooner or Later*, hosted *Solid Gold*, played the title character in the ABC series *Streethawk* and guest-starred on *Fairytale Theatre, Cagney and Lacey, Murder, She Wrote* and *Houston Nights*. For the silver screen he appeared in *Headin' for Broadway* and the soon-to-be-released *Transformations*.

ICE CREAM DREAM CAKE   page 195

LEWIS J. STADLEN

Lewis J. Stadlen made his Broadway debut portraying Groucho Marx in *Minnie's Boys* for which he received the Outer Critics' Circle, Drama Desk and Theatre World Awards. He originated the role of Ben Silverman in Neil Simon's *The Sunshine Boys* and played Voltaire and Dr. Pangloss, among other characters, in *Candide* for which he was nominated for the Tony. He also appeared on Broadway as Manolo in the female version of *The Odd Couple* with Rita Moreno and as Mendel in *Fiddler on the Roof*. Some of his other stage credits include *The Time of Your Life* with Henry Fonda, *Olympus on My Mind, 1-2-3-4-5!* with Vicki Lewis and the title roles in *Semmelweiss* and *The Last Days of Issac, The Miser* at Yale Rep and *Orpheus in the Underworld* for the Houston Grand Opera. Mr. Stadlen has appeared in the feature films *The Verdict, To Be or Not to Be, Serpico, Between the Lines, Savages* and *Portnoy's Complaint*. He was nominated for the Emmy Award for his performance as Samuel Leibowitz in *Judge Horton and the Scottsboro Boys*, and has also been seen on *Benson* and *The Equalizer*.

FRANCES STERNHAGEN

Frances Sternhagen won the 1974 Tony Award for her performance in *The Good Doctor* and has been nominated, in total, five times to date. Other Broadway plays in which she has appeared include *Equus, On Golden Pond, You Can't Take it With You* and *Home Front*. She has received the Clarence Derwent, the Drama Desk and two Obie Awards. Off-Broadway Miss Sternhagen has been seen in *Misalliance, The Pinter Plays, Little Murders* and *Driving Miss Daisy*, to name a few. Her recent feature films include *Bright Lights, Big City, See You in the Morning* and *Communion* with Christopher Walken. The most recent of her television appearances include *Resting Place, At Mother's Request* and *Cheers*.

ELAINE STRITCH

Elaine Stritch is the multi-talented actress of stage, screen and television in both the United States and London. She spent thirteen years of her professional career playing in major productions in the West End. In addition to appearing in the London companies of the Broadway hits *Sail Away* and *Company*, Miss Stritch starred in *Small Craft Warnings*, *The Gingerbread Lady* and the extremely successful TV series *Two's Company* which has been rerun in this country. Her Broadway credits include: *Pal Joey*, *On Your Toes*, *Goldilocks*, *Sail Away* and *Company*, for which she was nominated for the Tony. Her motion picture career has been just as illustrious as her Broadway career. She has appeared in the classic *Farewell to Arms*, *Providence*, Woody Allen's *September* and, most recently, *Cocoon, the Return*. Miss Stritch is currently working on a new musical based on a Damon Runyon story.

SALLY STRUTHERS

Sally Struthers, who won two Emmy Awards for her work in *All in the Family*, has many outstanding television and movie roles to her credit. Her break came in 1967 in a Herb Alpert TV special. Miss Struthers appeared in the back row of the chorus line, in good company with Goldie Hawn. Before being discovered by Norman Lear she was a regular on *The Summer Brothers Smothers Show* and *The Tim Conway Comedy Hour*. A case of laryngitis was what won her the role of Gloria Stivic on *All in the Family*. The day she was to read for the show's creator/producer, Lear, she lost her voice but went to the audition anyway. The sound of her hoarse, raspy voice struck Lear as the funniest thing he had ever heard. He'd already known she could act, having spotted her in *Five Easy Pieces*. The crazy voice, which had nothing to do with the character, secured her the role. Miss Struthers hit the Broadway boards for the first time in 1981 in *Wally's Cafe* with Rita Moreno and James Coco. It was a wonderful debut and sparked her return in 1985 in the female version of *The Odd Couple*. She currently stars in the nationally syndicated *9 to 5* for the Fox Network. In 1976, she was named National Chairperson of the International Christian Children's Fund and in 1987, to the Fund's Board of Directors. She has visited the children she seeks to help in Guatemala, Thailand and Africa. Sally feels that world hunger can be conquered - one child at a time.

LYNNE TAYLOR-CORBETT

Lynne Taylor-Corbett has worked in theatre, film and dance as a choreographer and director. She co-directed *Boy's Breath* at La MaMa, wrote and directed *Hollywood Endings* for solo artist Ellen Kogan and directed *Mona Rogers in Person* at the Cherry Lane Theatre. On Broadway, she choreographed *Chess* and *Shakespeare's Cabaret*. Other stage work includes James Lapine's production of *Merrily We Roll Along* at the La Jolla Playhouse and Anthony Newley's recent production of *Stop the World*. Her film feats are represented in the Orion release *In the Crowd* and the Paramount feature *Footloose*. In concert, The Atlanta, The Pennsylvania, The Milwaukee and the Louisville Ballets have all presented her works. Her newest work, entitled *Hide and Seek*, was commissioned by Jennifer Muller's The Works and recently premiered in New York at The Joyce Theatre.

CHICKEN BREASTS a la D.J. TAYLOR   page 136
HOLIDAY JELLO MOLD   page 196

CATHERINE ULISSEY

Catherine Ulissey, born in New York and raised in Saudi Arabia, is an honors graduate of The National Academy of Arts. She began her career with the Maryland Ballet, was a soloist with The Iranian Contemporary Ballet, a Principal Dancer and Ballet Mistress for 7 years with The Feld Ballet and has performed as guest artist with The New York City Opera and Pilobolus. Once Miss Ulissey turned her sights to Broadway she could not go unnoticed. Her magnetic style won her spots in the Tony Award-winning *The Mystery of Edwin Drood*, the original company of *Rags* and as Meg Giry in Andrew Lloyd Webber's *The Phantom of the Opera*.

CARROT CAKE   page 189
BANANA NUT BREAD   page 203

BRENDA VACCARO

Brenda Vaccaro made her Broadway debut in 1961 in *Everybody Loves Opal* for which she won a Theatre World Award, followed by her first starring Broadway role in *The Affair*. Ms. Vaccaro has been nominated for three Tony Awards for her outstanding performances in *Cactus Flower, How Now Dow Jones* and *The Goodby People*. She appeared opposite Gene Hackman on Broadway in Irwin Shaw's *Children From Their Games*, starred in *Father's Day* and the female version of *The Odd Couple* with Sally Struthers. While performing in *How Now Dow Jones*, she landed her first motion picture role in Garson Kanin's *Where It's At* and, shortly after, was boosted to international stardom with her performance in *Midnight Cowboy*. Her film career continued with a stream of major films: *I Love My Wife* with Elliot Gould; *Summer Tree* with Michael Douglas; *Going Home* with Robert Mitchum and *Once is Not Enough* for which she received an Oscar nomination, a Golden Globe Award and People's Choice Award for Best Supporting Actress. Television audiences have seen her in countless movies, specials and series, including her own, *Sara*, which garnered an Emmy nomination. Other Emmy Award performances include the musical comedy review *The Shape of Things to Come* directed by Lee Grant and an episode of *St. Elsewhere*. Recent projects include the films *Super Girl*, the upcoming *Water* with Michael Caine, the TV series *Paper Dolls* and *Deceptions* with Stephanie Powers.

BRENDA'S MEATLOAF   page 153

JOYCE VAN PATTEN

Joyce Van Patten has starred on Broadway in three Neil Simon productions: *Rumors, I Ought to Be in Pictures* and *Brighton Beach Memoirs*. She has also appeared in Bernard Slade's *Same Time, Next Year*, Edgar Lee Masters' *Spoon River Anthology*, George Firth's *The Supporting Cast* and Chekhov's *The Seagull* for Joseph Papp's Public Theatre. Some of Miss Van Patten's television credits include *Malice in Wonderland, Under the Influence, Bus Stop* and *Ladies in Waiting*. Miss Van Patten has given fine performances in the films *St. Elmo's Fire, The Falcon and the Snowman, The Bad News Bears, Mame* and George Romero's *Monkey Shines*. Her screenplay *Would You Show Us Your Legs, Please* has recently been optioned by CBS.

GWEN VERDON

Gwen Verdon has sung, danced and acted her way to receiving four Tony Awards for performances in *Can Can*, *Damn Yankees*, *New Girl in Town* and *Redhead*, and two additional nominations for *Sweet Charity* and *Chicago*. She also appeared on Broadway in *Alive and Kicking* and *Children Children*. Her unmistakable style incorporates both vivaciousness and vulnerability and has led to a multitude of roles. In film, Miss Verdon has starred in *Damn Yankees*; *David and Bathsheba*; *Meet Me After the Show*; *The Farmer Takes a Wife* ; *Cocoon* and *Cocoon, the Return*. Some television appearances include: *Dear John*, *Webster* and *Magnum PI*, for which she was nominated for an Emmy Award. Two Donaldson Awards, a Front Page, Drama Critics' Circle, Dance Magazine, Theatre World, Grammy and Mother of the Year Awards are also to her credit.

GWEN VERDON'S BASIC OAT MUFFINS   page 206

CHRISTOPHER WALKEN

ROASTED TARRAGON CHICKEN   page 146

ELI WALLACH

Eli Wallach, a charter member of the Actors Studio, won the Tony Award as the original Mangiacavallo in Tennessee Williams' *The Rose Tattoo* and was featured in Williams' *Camino Real*. Since meeting his wife, Anne Jackson, in a production of *This Property is Condemned* at the Equity Library Theatre, Mr. Wallach and Miss Jackson have appeared together in numerous New York productions, some of which include: *The Typist and the Tiger, Luv, Twice Around the Park, Rhinoceros*, the hit revival of *Waltz of the Toreadors, The Diary of Anne Frank* and *Cafe Crown*, all on Broadway. On screen, Mr. Wallach has given many memorable performances in such major films as *Baby Doll, The Magnificent Seven, The Misfits, The Good, the Bad and the Ugly, Tough Guys* and *Nuts*. His hundreds of television appearances include roles in *The Executioner's Song, For Whom the Bell Tolls, Skokie, Kojak, Batman* and *Captain Kangaroo*.

BLACKENED SWORDFISH   page 130
EGGS BIRMINGHAM   page 212

B.D. WONG

B.D. Wong was born and raised in San Francisco and made his professional debut as Androcles in *Androcles and the Lion* at New York's Town Hall in 1982. After a move to Los Angeles, B.D. appeared on television in the made for TV film *Crash Course* and the series *Blacke's Magic, Simon and Simon, Shell Game, Hard Copy* and *Sweet Surrender*, as well as the feature film *The Karate Kid II*. Other theatrical credits include *See Below Middle Sea* for the Center Theatre Group's Taper, Too, the Coast Playhouse's Los Angeles premiere of *Gifts of the Magi* and in the world premiere of the musical *Mail*. Mr. Wong is proud to have performed in the second *Salute to Sondheim* benefit for AIDS Project Los Angeles, and recently acted out a personal fantasy at East/West Players in the first *A Chorus Line* cast entirely of Asian-American performers. While celebrating a Broadway debut for creating the role of Song Liling in *M. Butterfly* in 1988, B.D. Wong was honored with the Drama Desk, Outer Critics' Circle, Theatre World, Actor's Equity Clarence Derwent, and American Theatre Wing's Tony Awards.

NONNA'S GNOCCHI   page 115

About The Author

A.J. VINCENT

A.J. Vincent has two passions: cooking and the theatre. About two years ago he was looking for a way to combine the two and the idea for *The Broadway Celebrity Cookbook* was born. The project got underway while Mr. Vincent was appearing in the Off-Broadway hit *Vampire Lesbians of Sodom*. Some of his other New York credits include: *Did You Ever Go to P.S. 43?*, *Girls We Have Known*, *Psycho Beach Party* and the concertized versions of *Miss Liberty*, with Tammy Grimes and Anita Gillette, and *Sadie Thompson*, with Ann Reinking and John McMartin. A.J. has performed regionally in *The Fantasticks*, *The Good Doctor*, *Dames at Sea* and in the premiere of Mark Zagoren's comedy *Princess Grace and the Fazzaris* at the Pittsburgh Public Theater. He has been seen in over a dozen national commercials and countless print ads and magazines. He is an honors graduate of Temple University and studied voice at the Wisconsin Conservatory of Music. Mr. Vincent has appeared on the daytime drama *Another World* and can be seen regularly as Lyle on *As the World Turns*.

HOMEMADE PASTA SAUCE   page 119
APPLE CRISP   page 188

Soups & Starters

The Bosco Antipasto
Patricia's Garlic Cheese Roll
Mom's Chili
Vegetarian Chili
Hot Curried Crab Dip
Helen Hayes' Curry Mousse
Fresh Mushroom Salad
Herbed Polenta with Fontina and Wild Mushrooms
Smoked Salmon a la Van Patten
Fresh Egg Noodles for a Big Pot of Chicken Soup
Liza's Gazpacho
Gazpacho-Rue
Oyster Stew
Tomato Masquerade
Vichyssoise

This Italian Antipasto has become a tradition (and closely held secret until now) at most of the cast parties my wife, Nancy, and I have held over the past 30 years. It started as a rather simple affair when my father put together two cheeses, salami and roasted red peppers. However, when my wife got her hands on it, it grew like Topsy to accomodate any number of people from two to a hundred. I have a penchant for casually inviting extra people to our parties and not telling Nancy until the night before. Our children do this also. Nancy automatically cooks for 20 more than the official "count."

In 1968, Lee J. Cobb, back in California after playing King Lear, sent me a telegram upon the opening of In The Matter of J. Robert Oppenheimer. *It read: "Desperate for antipasto recipe. Must Have. Please send. Good luck with play."*

In 1977, at our St. Joan *cast party, Lynn Redgrave was spied writing the list of ingredients on a scrap of paper as she tasted each one. Ten years later she came to another of our parties and declared herself "enraptured" with this dish again. However, she didn't ask for the recipe.*

So many people over the years have wanted this recipe that we have finally decided to give it up to the world. May everyone enjoy the gastronomical event of this dish, as we have.

-Philip Bosco

THE BOSCO ANTIPASTO
serves a party

Genoa salami	pickled peppers
hard salami	sweet roasted peppers
pepperoni	fresh green and/or red peppers
Provalone Cheese	black olives
Ricotta cheese	ceci beans
Mozzarella salad cheese	fresh tomatoes
plain, canned artichoke hearts	anchovies (optional)
fresh oregano and basil	cold-pressed virgin olive oil

The quantity of the ingredients depends entirely on the cook's preferences and the number of people to be fed. It is incredibly simple to prepare. Cut the meats, cheeses, peppers and tomatoes into bite-sized pieces, mix. Add the artichokes, olives, ceci beans and anchovies, toss well. Mix the spices with the olive oil and pour over the salad just before serving.

This whole thing can be cut and mixed on a large platter if serving only 4 to 8 people, or mixed in a restaurant-sized stainless steel bowl for the gangs of people who usually eat in our house. This list of ingredients is standard for us, but any number of variations are possible. It is a hit every time we do it - a "theatrical" dish for people who like bold and exciting food.

My two sisters, Mary and Patricia, can cook. I rarely try. They've raised kids and have cooked delicious meals for their families and guests over the years. My favorite foods to eat and prepare are appetizers. This one has become a Christmas tradition in our family. It will keep throughout the holidays; great for snacking.

-Kathy Bates

PATRICIA'S GARLIC CHEESE ROLL

1 lb Blue cheese
1 lb Cream cheese
1/2 cup finely chopped pecans
2 cloves garlic, pressed
Tabasco
Worchestershire Sauce
chili powder, for covering

Let the cheeses stand until they are room temperature. Mash and mix in all the ingredients (Tabasco and Worchestershire to taste). Form into a roll and roll in chili powder. Chill before serving. Serve with melba rounds or crackers.

My mom's chili (along with mashed potatoes and salad) was a favorite meal of mine after high school football or basketball practice at the end of a cold and exhausting autumn or winter day in Cleveland. My mother fed a family of six -four boys, and somehow her foods seemed to convey the essence of family, caring and community.

-David Birney

MOM'S CHILI
serves 4-6

11/2 lbs ground steak or chuck
2 16oz cans kidney beans, rinsed
1 can tomato soup and 1 can water
1 green pepper, finely chopped
1 small onion, finely chopped
1 Tbs sugar
2 Tbs chili powder (or to taste)
1 Tbs cornstarch

Brown ground beef in a little oil together with onion and green pepper until vegetables are tender. Add the kidney beans, soup, water, and chili powder. Simmer for one hour, stir frequently.

In a small bowl, mix the cornstarch with a little water. Stir until it makes a paste. Add to chili a bit at a time to thicken.

Serve with Cornbread or Irish Soda Bread (pg. 205)

I always hated chili until I discovered this recipe of Jeanne Jones' at the Canyon Ranch in Tuscon, Arizona. This wonderful concoction can burn off calories as the chili powder tickles your tongue. Remember, "A lean horse runs a long race." Keep thin and fit!
                                                                    -Tovah Feldshuh

VEGETARIAN CHILI
serves 6-8

2 cups chopped onions
2 tsp finely chopped garlic cloves
1/2 cup canned green chilies, chopped
2 cups diced tomatoes
2 tsp oregano, crushed with a mortar and pestle
2 tsp cumin
2 1/2 tsp chili powder
6 cups red kidney beans

Place the onion and garlic in a large saucepan. Cover and cook over low heat until soft, stirring frequently to avoid burning. Add all other ingredients except the kidney beans, mix thoroughly. Allow to come to a slow simmer before adding the kidney beans. Add the drained kidney beans and let cook for 20 to 30 more minutes. Stir often from the bottom of the pot.

Each serving contains approximately 205 calories.

Kathy Bates
HOT CURRIED CRAB DIP

1 medium green pepper, chopped
3 green onions, chopped
2 cans condensed cream of mushroom soup
2 small cans crabmeat, drained
2 eggs, well beaten
3 Tbs chopped pimentos
2 Tbs curry powder

Sauté the green pepper and onions in butter until tender. Add the soup and bring to a boil. Add the crabmeat and allow to boil for two minutes. Remove from heat and stir in the eggs, pimentos and curry powder. Serve in a chafing dish with melba rounds.

This dish does well for a light lunch on a hot day or for cocktails with melba toast.
-Helen Hayes

HELEN HAYES' CURRY MOUSSE
serves 6-8

6 hard boiled egg yolks
2 cups chicken broth
2 packages of plain gelatin softened in 1/2 cup cold water
11/2 cups mayonnaise
curry to taste (I like it hot)
1 drop Tabasco

Put it all in the blender and blend well. Pour into a one quart mold and refrigerate until firm or over night. When set, remove from mold onto a decorative plate and garnish as desired. I like to use a round cake pan with a center hole into which I put fresh watercress.

I personally made new friends... just with this recipe. After all, the best way to an audience's heart is through it's stomach!

-Jean LeClerc

FRESH MUSHROOM SALAD

large white mushrooms (4 to 5 per person)
scallions, finely chopped
juice of 1 or 11/2 lemons
one bunch parsley, finely chopped
salt and pepper
a touch of fine herbs
one cup of heavy cream (refrigerated)

Mix everything with a wooden spoon and serve chilled with white wine.

Great appetizer!!!

Jaclyn Oddi, Head Chef, Orso Restaurant
HERBED POLENTA WITH FONTINA AND WILD MUSHROOMS
(Polenta All'erbe con Fontini e Funghi)
serves 4

6 cups water
salt
11/2 cups corn meal
1 Tbs thyme and sage, roughly chopped
2oz grated Parmesan
4oz mixed, wild mushrooms, sliced
2 tsp butter
2 Tbs Marsala wine
1 Tbs unsalted butter
6oz Fontina, grated

For the polenta: Bring the water with 2 tsp salt to a boil. Through your fingers, sieve in the corn meal. Stir constantly. When the meal is incorporated reduce heat to a simmer. Continue stirring until the polenta pulls away from the sides of the pan (about 20 minutes) then stir in the chopped thyme and sage, and the 2 oz of grated Parmesan. Pull the polenta out of the pot and form into a square 1/2 inch thick on a wet board or counter. When cool, cut into 4 squares.

In a medium pan, sauté the mushrooms in 2 tsp butter. After 30 seconds add the Marsala wine and let the alcohol burn off. Set aside.

In a large non-stick skillet, melt 1 Tbs unsalted butter. Brown the polenta on one side, turn over and sprinkle each square with 11/2 oz Fontina. Broil until cheese is melted. Divide the mushrooms evenly on top of the Fontina and continue to broil until mushrooms are hot.

Both my mother and step-mother were expert cooks. They rarely used recipes. They invented delicious treats for all occasions. I've started many a dinner party with this simple one. People always seem to love it - there is no preparation time - lots of pluses. This particular dish came from my step-mother, Elenore Della Satta Van Patten.

-Joyce Van Patten

SMOKED SALMON a la VAN PATTEN

smoked Salmon, 2 slices per person
1 large red onion, sliced in thin rounds
1 small jar of capers
1 lemon
freshly ground black pepper
extra virgin olive oil

Lay the 2 slices of smoked Salmon on each individual plate (the Salmon should be thinly sliced). Cover the Salmon with the onion slices and capers. Squeeze the lemon over it, sprinkle with black pepper, dribble sparingly with a very good olive oil (should not be too oily). Serve with slices of Pumpernickel bread and sweet butter.

I don't cook much, but these noodles are the best thing I make. They are delicious when dropped into a simmering pot of chicken broth.

-John McMartin

FRESH EGG NOODLES
for Homemade Chicken Soup
yields 3 cups

1/2 tsp salt
2 cups flour
2 eggs slightly beaten

Mix and sift flour and salt. Gradually add to the eggs until a stiff dough is formed. Knead on a floured board. Roll to 1/16 inch thickness. Dry thoroughly by placing rolled dough on a tea towel over the back of a straight chair. Cut the dough into 1/4 inch wide strips or fancy shapes.

★ ☆ ★

A BIG POT OF CHICKEN SOUP
serves 1 person with a bad cold *or*
8 healthy appetites

2 whole chicken breasts
4 quarts water
2 tsp salt
1 Tbs pepper
2 cups celery, chopped
1 cup carrot, shredded
2 medium onions, diced
3 cups homemade noodles (optional)

Put the chicken breasts into a big pot filled with water. Salt and pepper. Bring to the boiling point; cover and simmer gently for about 2 hours. Every so often skim the top of the water with a tea strainer to remove any build up. When the chicken breasts have cooked sufficiently, take them from the pot, skin and debone them and cut into 1/2 inch strips. Return strips to the stock. Add the vegetables and allow to simmer until they are tender. Be sure the stock is boiling before adding the noodles. Add the noodles and cook for 15 minutes longer or until noodles are tender.

Liza Minnelli
LIZA'S GAZPACHO
serves 8-10

5 cucumbers, peeled and seeded
1 medium onion
2 slices white bread
2 10oz cans tomato juice
1 small can peeled tomatoes
3/4 cup olive oil
1 lemon, peeled and seeded
2 green peppers, skin only
2 egg yolks
3 cups water
2 dashes Tabasco
salt and pepper to taste

Purée all the ingredients in a blender. Chill and serve.

In Spain, Gazpacho is made with half a loaf of bread blended into the soup. It's thick and delicious. In the US, we add the bread over the top. It's lower in calories and, also delicious. This recipe is my modification of one I got in Cadiz while making an Agatha Christie TV movie, Summer of 1988, from my hotel chef. (I gained 4 pounds.)

-Rue McClanahan

GAZPACHO-RUE
serves 4

2 large ripe tomatoes
1 large sweet pepper
1 clove garlic
1/2 cup mixed: chives, parsley, basil and tarragon
1/2 cup vegetable oil
3 Tbs lemon juice
3 cups chilled water or light chicken stock
1 medium onion, thinly sliced
1 cup diced cucumber
11/2 tsp salt substitute
1/2 tsp paprika
1/2 cup crumbled bread pieces
1 Tbs parsley, chopped

Remove the membrane from the sweet pepper and tomatoes, peel the garlic, wash the herbs. Chop all together in a large bowl. Stir in the oil, lemon juice and water. Add the onion, cucumber, salt substitute and paprika. Blend well in a blender. Chill for at least four hours. Add parsley, sprinkle the top of each bowl with bread bits and serve.

★ ☆ ★

I can't stand people who say they don't like oysters and they've never SEEN an oyster. Now here is a positively captivating, simple, anyone-can-do-it, oyster stew that warms the cockles of the heart and your toenails, too.

-Phyllis Diller

OYSTER STEW
serves 2

Melt 2 Tbs butter in a sauce pan. Dump in contents of a small can of small oysters. Dump in juice and all. Bring to a boil. Add 2 cups low fat milk, salt and pepper.

Remove from fire and serve piping hot with oyster crackers. Oh, hot damn!

Harvey Schmidt
TOMATO MASQUERADE
serves 2

1 can Campbell's Tomato Soup
Half and Half or heavy cream
1 real tomato
1 small, but real, onion, crudely chopped
chives, crudely chopped
freshly cracked black peppercorns

Open can of soup and pour contents into saucepan. Fill the empty can with either Half and Half or heavy cream. Pour slowly into saucepan, stirring all the while. Chop the whole, real tomato into chunky hunks and drop it all, including seeds and juice, into saucepan. Heat slowly, stirring occasionally, allowing a few extra moments at the end to simmer. Pour contents from saucepan into twin, heavy glass, Bavarian goblets from Tiffany & Co. Crack peppercorns liberally into each goblet, then sprinkle the chopped onion and chives excessively on top. Serve with perversely tiny open-faced grilled cheese sandwiches. In the event additional servings are required (and they usually are), feel free to begin with several cans of soup, and increase all other ingredients accordingly.

My mother was an expert at putting together lovely, low cost meals during the Great Depression. I have inherited her zeal for beating the high cost of eating. Here is my recipe for Vichyssoise.

-Phyllis Diller

VICHYSSOISE

Make chicken broth with bouillon crystals. Add same amount of buttermilk. Serve chilled with chopped scallions and/or chives sprinkled on top. Because of the salt content in the boullion, just add pepper, if you like.

Pasta & Fish

Clam Do
Fettuccine Botto
Fettuccine Ferrer
Nonna's Gnocchi
Nickie's Anchovy Pasta
Pasta with Broccoli and Sun Dried Tomatoes
Pasta Carbonara
Homemade Pasta Sauce
Perciatelli with Tomato/Anchovy Sauce
Joel Grey's Riso Alfredo
Spaghetti and Meat Sauce
A Stritch in Dine
Taglierini with Smoked Trout and Sun Dried Tomatoes
Szechuan Cold Noodles in Sesame Sauce
Lobster Salad with Basil and Lemon Dressing
Fairy Pudding
Steam-Broiled Fish
Nick's Flaky Fish Fillets
Blackened Swordfish

I'm really not a cook; certainly not a creative one; usually a hurried one. This recipe is quick and easy. I discovered it by accident when I realized it was Friday and I'd planned on Spaghetti and Meat Sauce. I was a little apprehensive because, you know kids (What's This? Yuck!), but they loved it! One of their picky little friends actually asked me for the recipe when she was eleven.

-Frances Sternhagen

CLAM DO
serves 4

2 8oz boxes spaghetti
4 small cans minced clams
1 to 2 Tbs olive oil
1 medium onion, chopped
2 stalks celery, chopped
1 clove garlic, pressed
1/2 to 3/4 box frozen spinach
1 small can water chestnuts, diced, for crunch

Cook the spaghetti and spinach according to package directions.

In a large skillet, heat the olive oil and sauté onion, celery and garlic until translucent.

Open cans of clams and drain out 1/2 of the liquid. Add clams, with remaining juice, water chestnuts and spinach to the skillet. Stir and spoon over cooked pasta.

This recipe can and should be adjusted to taste. Use more or less of the water chestnuts and box of spinach.

My mother and father were born in a small village in Northern Italy called Camandona. One of our relatives, a madame D'Agostino (no relation to the store), taught my mother how to cook. One of her specialties was Fettuccine Botto. My mother, in turn, passed this recipe on to my sister who has been concocting it, with great success, ever since our mother passed away.

-Louis Botto

FETTUCCINE BOTTO
serves 4-6

1/4 lb (one stick) butter
1 cup heavy cream
sea salt
freshly ground black pepper
1 clove garlic, chopped
5 carrots
1/2 lb prosciutto, cut the width of the fettuccine
1 lb spinach fettuccine
1 cup freshly grated Parmesan cheese

Keys to success: All ingredients must be absolutely FRESH. The fettuccine should be homemade; however, since we don't want to miss the first act, we will buy excellent "homemade" fettuccine at our local Italian deli (Cannillo's in West New York, New Jersey). Prosciutto should be lean and tender. All ingredients should be at room temperature. Use only wooden spoons for turning the ingredients, which should be done gently.

Preparation: Scrape, wash and cut the carrots into 3 inch pieces equal to the width of the fettuccine. Steam the carrots in a steaming basket, in one inch of water, for two minutes. Set aside.

Use a heavy pan large enough to eventually hold all the ingredients. Melt the butter in this pan over very low heat. Before the butter begins to simmer add the heavy cream and chopped garlic. Heat until it begins to simmer and immediately turn off the heat.

Prepare the pasta according to your taste; I enjoy it "al dente." Drain well and turn carefully into the sauce over medium heat. Be sure the pasta is completely coated and add all remaining ingredients, heating for no longer than 2 minutes. Serve hot with fresh grated cheese on the side.

*This is what I like to cook on Sundays when my time is my own and I don't have to be at
the theatre.*

-Jose Ferrer

FETTUCCINE FERRER
serves 4

1 lb fresh fettuccine noodles
1/3 cup plus 2 tsp virgin olive oil
2 garlic cloves
1/3 cup pine nuts
1 cup canned whole tomatoes, peeled, seeded and chopped
1 cup canned tuna, either in water or oil
10 black olives, sliced
1/2 red pimento, cut into strips
11/2 Tbs parsley, chopped
2 Tbs red wine vinegar
freshly ground coriander

Cook fettuccine in water with 1/2 tsp salt and 2 tsp olive oil added. Drain and set
aside when pasta is tender.

Heat the oil in a large skillet. Chop the garlic very fine. Sauté the garlic and pine
nuts over low heat until the garlic is clear and the pine nuts are a golden color.
Add the chopped tomatoes, cook briefly so the tomatoes lose their bitterness
(about 30 seconds). Pour into a decorative serving bowl and set aside to cool.

Add the cooked pasta to the tomato/pine nut sauce and toss. Add the remaining
ingredients with the exception of the coriander. Turn gently. Salt and pepper to
taste. At the table, dish out each serving and sprinkle each with a dash of
coriander. Serve at room temperature.

I recently had an exquisite Valentine's Day late supper at a restaurant called Texarkana, which I often passed when I first came to New York around 1982. Alas, as a rather struggling actor, I recall it seemed so expensive; I couldn't entertain the idea of eating out at all, let alone expensively. While I sat savoring this fabulous meal, a song came from the stereo at the bar that I hadn't heard since those lean old days, "Boogie Down" by Al Jarreau. In those days I shared an apartment in a very bizzare building on 42nd St and Eighth Avenue (above part of "the largest adult entertainment complex in the world") with two aspiring actresses, Lyn Vaux and Karen Sullivan, who both cooked like you always dreamed at least one of your roomates would. Though we ate modestly, we ate marvelously. As we aspired we all agreed that whoever got a job would splurge; shop and prepare their own celebratory meal for all, perhaps a step above our usual modest fair. Lyn, having passed a Ninth Avenue fishseller one day, fantasized how that meal might include Red Snapper. From that day on Red Snapper became the household symbol for the successful thespian. Whenever one of us had an important morning audition the other two would put Al Jarreau's "Boogie Down" on the stereo, blast it, and dance a kind of tribal dance of encouragement around the auditionee. This continued out into the hall with the front door wide open, and to the elevator where, as the elevator doors closed, the other two (usually pajama-ed or be-robed) hooted, stomped, and finally hollared, "Make it a Red Snapper Day!!!" Whatever it was, it worked. When you were the one in the elevator, you always felt so confident, so talented, so loved. I'll never forget it.

When it was finally my turn to actually make Red Snapper, I had just gotten the part of Benjamin in Joseph and the Amazing Technicolor Dreamcoat *at a dinner theatre in Elmsford, NY. I baked the Red Snapper, I think, and made an extra special version of our favorite tossed green ("oooh...Romaine!") and because it was an extra special night, I made Karen's grandmother's Gnocchi, which Karen had taught me to make when we were in high school. I tossed some with a red sauce, and some with butter and parmesan and, because I shared this candlelit evening with my steadfast buds in such celebration, I don't think anything ever tasted better.*

I dedicate this entry of Karen's "Nonna" Maria Azzolino's Gnocchi recipe to all the Sullivans for the gift of their daughter and sister, her·friendship and for their love, which has always made me feel like a successful actor and person.

Texarkana? Well, I had to keep myself from crying there. Was it the heavenly food? The brilliant service? My glorious Valentine companion? Or was it the voice of Al Jarreau, my mere presence in a once unaffordable restaurant, and the memory of precious salad days I'll never have again? Who knew? I just sang along with Al.

"I can be
what I want
and all I need is to get my boogie down."

Make it a Red Snapper Day.

-B.D. Wong

NONNA'S GNOCCHI
serves 4

3 medium potatoes; boiled, drained and mashed
salt
3-4 cups flour
1 egg, slightly beaten

When mashed potatoes are lukewarm, start mixing in flour a cup at a time, then the egg, making a dough that is soft but not sticky. Knead on a floured surface, but don't knead too long. The dough will absorb flour quite a bit depending on the potatoes. Break off a fist sized piece and roll into thumb diameter coils. Break off into 1" pieces. Roll each piece on a floured surface toward the body, making an indentation with the distal portion of your fingers. You'll just have to see it done once.

Place finished gnocchi on towels. Cook in plenty of boiling, salted water for 4-5 minutes.

I usually take them out with a slotted spoon as they begin to float. Toss them with something that tastes really good.

I've never written a recipe before, but I try to copy my favorite pastas from restaurants. I copied this one from a place down the street from a theatre I played in Miami Beach.

-Bebe Neuwirth

NICKIE'S ANCHOVY PASTA
serves 2

1 lb pasta of your choice
1 clove garlic, crushed and minced
1 can anchovies, sliced into 1/2 inch pieces
3 Tbs olive oil
sweet basil

As the water for the pasta is heating to a boil:

Heat a 9" skillet and coat the bottom of the pan with the olive oil. Keep the pan moving and as the oil starts to thin add the garlic. When the garlic is halfway to golden add the anchovies. When the garlic is 3/4 of the way to golden, add about 11/2 Tbs of sweet basil flakes. Stir throughout with a wooden utensil. Hopefully when the garlic is golden brown, the pasta is al dente.

Drain the pasta and spoon onto two warmed plates. Pour the sauce over and toss.

For those people who hate anchovies, make this dish the same way without the little fish. Use any shape pasta. Penne and Rotelle however, are very good at holding sauce. This, believe it or not, will be great cold tomorrow.

★ ☆ ★

This is one of my favorite between show meals. It is so quick and easy to prepare, there is still plenty of time to relax before "half hour." It is full of healthy veggies and chock-full of energy boosting carbohydrates to get through that second show. Most important though, it's delicious!

-Marcia Mitzman

PASTA WITH BROCCOLI
AND SUN DRIED TOMATOES
serves 2

3 to 4 cups Ziti or Rigatoni
11/2 cups broccoli florets
5 Tbs olive oil
3 cloves crushed garlic
1/2 cup chopped onion (optional)
6 sun dried tomatoes, chopped
fresh, grated Parmesan cheese
fresh ground pepper

Sauté garlic and onion in olive oil over a low flame until tender and slightly brown. Steam the broccoli until tender and set aside. Meanwhile, cook the pasta (al dente). Just before the pasta is done, add the broccoli to the garlic, onion and oil and sauté over a low flame for 1 minute. Drain the pasta, add it to the broccoli mixture. Add the sun dried tomatoes and toss lightly for one minute.

Serve with fresh Parmesan and black pepper.

Top off the meal with a loaf of Italian bread and a jug of your favorite wine.

There was a great scene in the movie Heartburn *where Merryl Streep and Jack Nicholson were eating Pasta Carbonara in bed after their first date. My husband thought it looked so good (the Pasta, that is) he begged me to make it for him. Funny, the recipe wasn't in the book* Heartburn *although others from the movie were. So I invented this one. Each time it turns out a bit differently because precise measurements are not important... experiment! I have found this dish to be fabulous comfort food. It can always soothe a late night craving because you probably have all the ingredients on hand.*

-Liz Callaway

PASTA CARBONARA
for 2 HUNGRY people

1/2 lb spaghetti noodles, preferably fresh
5 slices regular bacon (or 3 slices of uncooked Canadian Bacon), diced
3 eggs
2 Tbs heavy cream
1/2 cup grated Parmesan cheese
3 Tbs fresh parsley, chopped
salt and pepper to taste

Cook pasta according to directions. During the 6 to 12 minutes that takes, cook the diced bacon in a large skillet (non-stick if possible) until done but not crisp. Meanwhile, in a medium sized bowl, beat the eggs together with the cream. Add the Parmesan cheese and blend until there are no lumps.

By this time, the pasta should be through cooking. Drain, add it to the skillet with the bacon and mix thoroughly. Over a low heat, pour the egg and cheese mixture into the pan of pasta. Toss lightly to coat, turn off heat. Sprinkle with parsley and mix. Salt and pepper to taste.

The pasta can be transferred to warmed plates and topped with a bit more Parmesan, fresh ground black pepper and VOILA!

When I was growing up, I spent a lot of time in the kitchen with either my mother or grandmother as they tended the spaghetti sauce as if it were being nurtured with every turn of the wooden spoon. The making of "gravy," as it was called in all the Italian households in my neighborhood, was an all-day, somewhat magical, affair. The time would fly by as I listened to stories that began "When I was young...," or "Did I ever tell you...?" The smells filled the house, my mind was wild with images of my family members in their youth and my fascination with cooking was spawned. I learned many a valuable lesson at the side of those loving women. I often spend an entire Saturday turning the sauce every 15 minutes, reliving those childhood days and thinking how rich my life is because of them. Although I don't start with whole fresh tomatoes and grind and strain them, I think I have come up with gravy that both my mother and Nannie would be proud of.

-A.J. Vincent

HOMEMADE PASTA SAUCE
enough for 6 meals-that's the only way I can make it!

olive oil
2 cloves garlic, whole
1 12oz can tomato paste
2 28oz cans tomato puree
2 28oz cans tomato sauce
1 28oz can whole, peeled, Italian tomatoes
1/4 cup dried oregano
1/4 cup dried parsley
OR 1/3 cup fresh parsley, finely chopped
3 whole bay leaves
2 Tbs dried basil
2 Tbs black pepper, or to taste
salt to taste
1 large onion
1 red pepper, cut in half and deveined
1 green pepper, cut in half and deveined
3 stalks celery including greens
1 wooden spoon, it won't taste the same without it

11/2 lbs hot Italian sausage
11/2 lbs sweet Italian sausage
1/2 stick pepperoni, skinned and cut in nickle slices
4 pork chops

First prepare yourself mentally to spend the day in the house near the stove. This may not sound like fun but it is. Plan on cleaning out a closet or doing a lot of laundry while the sauce is cooking. You'll get into it.

In a very large pot, heat 21/2 Tbs olive oil over medium heat and cook the garlic for about two minutes. Fry the tomato paste until it turns a dark red color. Be sure it does not burn. Add half can of water. Reduce heat. Add the puree and sauce, stir so that the paste is well incorporated. Rinse out each can with half can of water and add to the pot.

Strain the whole tomatoes, add pulp and juice (but no seeds) to the sauce.

Add all the spices and vegetables, stir. Cover the pot with a crooked lid. Stir every 15 minutes, from the bottom, so it doesn't stick and burn. The heat level will have to be watched carefully and adjusted. The sauce should maintain a slow simmer. Water may need to be added from time to time so the sauce doesn't get too thick. Add about 1/4 cup, stir, and see if that helps.

In a skillet boil the sausage in enough water to just cover meat, until it turns whitish. Drain, brown, cut into large pieces and set aside. In the same pan brown the pepperoni, set aside. Brown the pork chops, set aside. After the sauce has been simmering for at least 4 hours, add the meat and some of the drippings. Stir.

Remove and discard the celery and bay leaves. Remove the onion, peppers and garlic and purée in a blender. Return the vegetable puree to the pot. Stir. During the next two hours the sauce will take on a deep red color, the whole house will fill with a hearty aroma and your gravy will have simmered to perfection. Serve over any pasta. Store the rest in containers and freeze. You'll eat like a king for weeks.

Unfortunately, I am a disaster in the kitchen. I can create a crisis just by heating up water, although I have finally gotten the knack of that. So I best stay with the naming of my favorite dish. I love Italian food and pasta in particular. My favorite pasta is Perciatelli. This, as you know, can best be described as a "swollen" spaghetti. Oddly enough a lot of Italian restaurants do not carry this, but I have found a few that do and I often go to these in New York City and on Long Island. I usually order it with a meat sauce, but I also had it with a very subtle anchovy-based sauce. To my taste, the taste and texture of Perciatelli, with the appropriate sauce, is a most rewarding meal. I rarely deviate from ordering this dish along with a salad.

-Morton Gould

This quick and easy sauce is the perfect compliment to Perciatelli or any plump pasta.

-Editor

TOMATO/ANCHOVY SAUCE
serves 4

2 Tbs olive oil
2 garlic cloves, chopped
1 2oz tin anchovy fillets, drained and chopped
1 28oz can whole tomatoes, seeded
1/2 cup chopped, fresh parsley

In a saucepan, heat the oil and sauté garlic until tender. Add the chopped anchovies and tomatoes. Raise the heat a bit to bring the sauce to a boil. Stir constantly to break up tomatoes. Just as the sauce boils reduce heat and simmer 20 minutes or until the sauce thickens. Add the chopped parsley and pour over 1 lb of Perciatelli.

★ ☆ ★

Joel Grey
JOEL GREY'S RISO ALFREDO
serves 4

1 box of DiCecco brand (riso) pasta
1 stick (1/4 lb) unsalted butter
1 pint heavy cream
1/2 lb chunk of Reggiano Parmesan cheese
1/2 lb grated Reggiano Parmesan cheese
fresh ground pepper
sweet and hot sausages
arrugula and fresh tomatoes
virgin olive oil (green) and balsamic vinegar

Cook 1 lb box of pasta in salted water as per directions on package. Taste during cooking until "al dente" rather than relying on time.

Reduce 1 pint of heavy cream about 1/3, and towards end of reduction add up to 1 stick of butter (depending on degree of richness desired), stirring in a large sauce pan over low heat.

When pasta is "al dente," stir same in fine strainer to remove water and add to the cream/butter mixture. Remove pan from stove. Dish will be very wet and in moments the riso will start to absorb the mixture to a consistancy similar to breakfast cereals like oatmeal, farina, etc. Add 1/2 lb grated Reggiano Parmesan cheese to the mixture and stir through.

Transfer to a warm, white bowl and bring directly to table. Spoon large portions onto plates with a fresh grind of Reggiano Parmesan on top. Optional: garnish with shaved white truffles. Pass cheese for guests to add to taste.

Serve with a salad of arrugula and tomatoes with a dressing of olive oil, balsamic vinegar and a splash of fresh lemon juice.

For more of a dinner meal, serve with grilled Italian sausages.

For wine, serve a full-bodied Chardonnay-Acacia or Mondavi or a great French white like Marquis de la Guiche (Montrachet).

For dessert, serve Marcella Hazan's mascerated orange slices in their own juice (from her first cookbook).

My Spaghetti and Meat Sauce is great for a party of 15 or a mad week of eating for one.
-Ruth Buzzi

SPAGHETTI AND MEAT SAUCE
serves 12-15

2 medium sized packages of cut up chicken thighs
6 medium pork chops
2 small steaks (optional)
3/4 lb hot Italian sausage
3/4 lb sweet Italian sausage
2 large jars spaghetti sauce
1 6oz can tomato paste, same can filled with water
2 8oz cans tomato sauce
1/2 cup dry white wine
1 large clove garlic, chopped
1 medium yellow onion, finely chopped
2 Tbs oilve oil
salt and pepper to taste
3 1 lb packages spaghetti or macaroni

Skin and de-bone chicken, remove fat and bones from the pork chops. Cut all the meat into bite-sized pieces. In a large pan, heat the oil and cook the garlic without burning. Add the onion, cook until soft. Put the meat into the pan, cooking until all sides change color so the juices are sealed. Do not brown. Add the tomato paste, stir thoroughly and add one can of water. Lightly salt, heavily pepper. Add tomato sauce; stir and simmer about ten minutes. Add commercial spaghetti sauce and stir. Cook a bit and add the wine. Simmer for three hours.

Cook pasta according to package directions, drain and place in a huge bowl. Pour some sauce over, stir and serve.

I always remove the meat and place in a separate bowl. Leave as much sauce as possible in the pan. Also, after mixing the spaghetti with the sauce, place extra sauce in a gravy bowl for guests who like more sauce. I serve this with a big salad and bread, and guests go "ape!" The meats do wonders to any of the commercial jarred sauces they are added to, especially if cooked for at least 2 hours...let alone 3!!! Help!! Oh - don't forget to buy a good grated cheese.

P.S. My favorite macaroni is Rigatoni. You know - the big "tubes?!?!"

This is a recipe of my own devising. I've had it in the kitchen!

-Elaine Stritch

A STRITCH IN DINE

Get your hair done
Apply subtle make-up
Put on low-heeled shoes
Don designer jeans
Top off with a silk blouse and loose sweater.

Pick up the telephone and dial (212) 489-7212 for ORSO Restaurant. Reserve a table. Walk to 322 West 46th Street in Manhattan. Check your coat, sit down-back and relax.

Jaclyn Oddi, Head Chef, Orso Restaurant
TAGLIERINI WITH SMOKED TROUT AND SUN DRIED TOMATOES
(Taglierini con Trota Affumicata e Pomodori Secchi)
serves 4

16 oz fresh Taglierini
2 to 3 oz smoked trout, skinned, boned and meat torn into small pieces
2 heaping Tbs capers, rinsed
2 oz sun dried tomatoes - blanched in boiling water for 30 seconds, drained
        and chopped
1 bunch scallions, chopped
6 oz fish stock or clam juice
2 oz olive oil
1 large clove garlic, minced
2 oz unsalted butter

Have at least 11/2 gallons salted water boiling for the pasta.
In a large skillet, heat the olive oil and sauté the garlic until it just begins to color.
Add the trout and tomatoes and sauté for 30 seconds. Add the fish stock, butter, capers and scallions. Raise heat and reduce slightly.
Cook the pasta, drain and pour into a heated bowl. Add the sauce and toss. Add extra butter and salt to taste.

★ ☆ ★

I've always had a weakness for this dish and order it in every Szechuan or Hunan restaurant I enter. Through trial and error I came up with this recipe. I use whole wheat pasta instead of Chinese noodles because they hold their texture better, as well as being healthier. I also use a sugar substitute to keep the calories down. This is a high protein, high fiber recipe perfect for people who care about such things. It's also great for vegetarians.

-Harvey Fierstein

SZECHUAN COLD NOODLES IN SESAME SAUCE
serves 4 as a main dish, 8 as a side dish

1 lb whole wheat pasta
1/4 cup natural peanut butter
1/4 cup tahini
2 Tbs sesame oil
4 garlic cloves
1 Tbs chili oil
scant tsp Szechuan peppercorns
1/4 cup sugar or substitute
1/2 cup soy sauce
1 tsp lemon juice
scallion slices for garnish

Boil pasta and allow to cool. Rinse under cold water. This does remove some of the vitamins but it keeps the pasta from sticking. Combine all other ingredients and blend thoroughly in a food processor using the metal blade. Pour sauce over pasta. Toss, garnish with scallion slices and serve.

The sauce can be prepared up to three days in advance and stored in the refrigerator. It tastes better with age.

This is a very simple but lovely lobster salad. Perfect for entertaining that important casting director on a hot summer day. Just make it beforehand and refrigerate, then garnish and serve without spending a minute slaving over a hot stove.

-Marcia Mitzman

LOBSTER SALAD
WITH BASIL AND LEMON DRESSING
serves 2

Two 11/2 lb live lobsters
1/2 cup fresh peas (frozen or canned will not do)
1/2 cup diagonally-cut celery pieces
1 Tbs fresh basil leaves, minced
1 Tbs lemon rind, grated
3 Tbs fresh lemon juice
1/3 cup olive oil
pepper to taste
tomato wedges, lemon slices and Bib lettuce for garnish

How to boil a lobster: Bring a large pot of salted water to a boil. Add the lobsters, cover the pot. Cook for eight minutes, starting your timer once the water returns to a boil.

Remove lobsters from the pot, set aside to cool.

Cook the peas in a small pan of water just until tender. Do not overcook. Drain and put in a large serving bowl. Stir in the celery, basil and the lemon rind.

Once the lobster has cooled, remove all the meat from the claws, tail and body and cut into 3/4" pieces. Add to the serving bowl and set aside while you prepare the dressing.

Dressing: In a small bowl whisk the lemon juice with a pinch of salt. Add the olive oil, in a constant stream, whisking all the while until it emulsifies.

Pour the dressing over the lobster, toss to coat evenly. Salt and pepper to taste.

Divide the salad between two plates and garnish with tomato wedges, lemon slices and Bib lettuce.

★ ☆ ★

When I first came to New York as a young dancer I happened to be fortunate enough to start working in Broadway musicals. Soon I became known as a full-time working gypsy. One of the very practical things I learned from the other dancers was how to make "Fairy Pudding." I could rush home from my dance class and make it. The recipe is one of my favorites.

-Dody Goodman

FAIRY PUDDING
serves 2

1 3oz can of tuna
1 can condensed mushroom soup
Heaping handful of unsalted potato chips

Dump tuna and mushroom soup into a casserole dish. Mix well. Bake in a 350° oven for 25 minutes. (Microwave for 7 minutes on HIGH.) Just before removing from the oven sprinkle potato chips over the top.

This is delicious served on a bed of rice with a green salad or steamed veggies. It gives one plenty of strength and energy to get through the show. Well, anyway, I like it. When I became a little more affluent, I would alternate with a broiled chicken breast stuffed with cream cheese. It's good!

I don't eat meat or salt. This recipe contains only fresh herbs and a bit of sesame oil. My recipes are very good for my diet which is one for arthritis. This particular dish is also good for keeping your weight down.

-Francesco Scavullo

STEAM-BROILED FISH

For The Stock
carrots, onions, celery, leeks

Ginger Marinade
large bunch of dill
large bunch of parsley
3 large cloves garlic
1 large piece ginger, peeled and cut
dash chili powder
1 medium onion
juice of 3 lemons

Fresh fish (one large fillet or steak per person). My favorites are: Grey Sole, Red Snapper, fresh Tuna and Bluefish.
sesame seeds

The fish derives its special moistness and flavor from the vegetable stock which can be made in large quantities and frozen.

Fill a stockpot with three or four each of: carrots, onions and leeks and a quartered bunch of celery with the leaves. Add peelings or trimmings from any vegetables you have available. Cover the vegetables with cold water, bring to a boil and immediately reduce the heat. Simmer for at least 12 hours. I keep the stockpot bubbling for up to 5 days, occasionally adding water and vegetables as necessary. Cool and strain into quart containers.

In a blender jar or food processor, combine all the marinade ingredients. Purée.

Arrange portions of fish in a shallow broiling pan. Pour marinade over fish then add vegetable stock to barely cover. Let fish marinate at room temperature for about an hour. Turn occasionally to allow marinade to permeate. When ready to cook, have broiler preheated to hottest setting. Sprinkle the fish with toasted, crushed sesame seeds.

Broil the delicate fillets for 10 minutes, baste frequently. If you have chosen the thicker fish, turn the pieces after 10 minutes and broil for an additional 8 minutes on the second side. Baste frequently! Serve at once, garnish with steamed, herbed vegetables (pg. 180) and a salad of sliced tomato and basil drizzled with a bit of extra virgin olive oil.

The Parmesan really makes this one. I'm not sure how I arrived at this specific recipe, but I probably, absent mindedly, tossed anything I could find on some fish. To make it more exciting, I grabbed the grated cheese and BINGO!

-Nick Kaledin

NICK'S FLAKY FISH FILLETS
serves 4

2 lbs fresh fillet of Sole
freshly ground black pepper
1/2 tsp paprika
flavored bread crumbs
4 Tbs grated Parmesan cheese
2 Tbs butter
lemon
parsley

Lightly butter a baking tray and lay in the fillets so they do not overlap. Dust with black pepper and paprika. Lightly sprinkle the tops with bread crumbs. Top off with a sprinkling of the Parmesan cheese (more than the bread crumbs). Place a pat of butter on each fillet and spritz with lemon.

Broil about 5 minutes or bake in a hot oven (400°) for slightly longer. Watch carefully they don't overcook and become dry.

Garnish with parsley sprigs and fresh lemon wedges. Goes well with rice or a baked potato and salad.

This recipe was taught to me by Danny Kaye. Danny was going to teach me a lot more about cooking before he left us.

-Eli Wallach

BLACKENED SWORDFISH

Draw the butter and brush the Swordfish. Place buttered Swordfish steaks in a heated skillet, after first coating with Prudhomme's New Orleans Flavor for Blackened Fish (or you can use other brands of Cajun flavoring). Turn over the steaks after 5 minutes. Be sure you make provisions for plenty of ventilation or you'll be smoked out of the kitchen. Serve with plenty of lemon slices.

Poultry

Chicken Alfredo
Chicken Alice Faye
Blythe's Chicken
Chicken Breasts a la D.J. Taylor
Cape Scott Chicken
Country Captain Chicken
My Fast Chicken
Nell Carter's Favorite Chicken
Buttermilk Fried Chicken
Nasi Goring
Quickest Chicken Dinner in the World
Reinking's Chicken and Dumplings
Chicken on the Road
Roasted Tarragon Chicken
Chicken a la Vicki

I don't eat this dish before a show as it has a heavy cream sauce with Parmesan cheese and doesn't help the singing! But it is wonderful on dark days and it is an impressive meal to guests. This is a very elegant entree but fairly easy to prepare. You can even make the chicken mixture ahead and keep in the fridge until you're ready to cook it.

-Marcia Mitzman

CHICKEN ALFREDO
serves 6

For the Chicken
1 lb boneless chicken breasts, trimmed
1 large egg yolk
11/2 cups heavy cream
salt & pepper

For the Alfredo Sauce
1/2 pint heavy cream
1/2 cup Parmesan cheese (a little more or less, add until sauce thickens)
2 to 3 tbs butter
fresh ground white pepper
dash ground coriander (optional)

Process the chicken breasts in a food processor using the metal blade. Add the egg yolk then gradually add the heavy cream while blending. Put the blended chicken and cream in a bowl and refrigerate for at least 30 minutes. After the 30 minutes has passed, form the chicken mixture into balls (about the size of a meatball) and drop into a pan of simmering water poaching until cooked. Do not overcook. Cut one open to check doneness if necessary. Set aside.

For the sauce: Pour the cream into a small, heavy saucepan. Heat over a low to medium flame. Add the butter and 1 Tbs Parmesan. Continue to heat and stir frequently. Try to maintain a light simmer. I've found the secret to a good Alfredo sauce is to heat it slowly, giving the cream time to thicken. As the sauce does thicken, add more Parmesan, fresh ground pepper and, maybe, a dash of coriander. The sauce is done when it coats the back of a spoon and doesn't run right off. When the sauce has thickened sufficiently, spoon it over the meatballs. If they have cooled then place them in the sauce for 1 minute. Serve 4 to 5 to each person.

To fill out the meal serve with a few colorful veggies. I think broccoli florets, glazed carrots and yellow squash make a pretty plate.

★ ☆ ★

Alice Faye and I became buddies during the New York rehearsals of the Broadway bound musical Good News. *In this revival she was sharing star billing with her old movie beau John Payne. It was being directed by Abe Burrows and I was helping with the choreography.*

Braving the "Big Apple" by herself, Alice came East without an entourage. When I asked her what she did after rehearsals, she replied, "I go back to the hotel." I then heard myself asking her over to dinner. I could have died when she said, "Sure, ...when?"

What would you serve for dinner if the Silver Screen's legendary Alice Faye was coming to your Westside tenement apartment?! She arrived in her block long silver limo; the neighbors were hanging out of their windows. They will never forget it and neither will I.

Alice is a great lady and a hell of a lot of fun. She also reminded me that she was born and reared in "Hell's Kitchen." Since this whole story reads like a movie script, it is only appropriate to note that whatever my chicken dish may have been called once upon a time, it has been Chicken Alice Faye happily ever after.

-Arthur Faria

CHICKEN ALICE FAYE
serves 2

2 whole, boneless chicken breasts
salt and pepper
all purpose flour
1/4 cup butter
1 Tbs shallots, finely chopped
3/4 cup dry white wine
1/2 tsp dried tarragon
1/3 cup chicken stock
1/4 cup heavy cream
Wondra flour

Salt and pepper the chicken and dredge in flour. Shake off the excess. Brown the chicken in 3 Tbs butter using a heavy fry pan. Remove and keep warm.

Sauté the shallots briefly in the same pan and add 1/4 cup wine. Cook over high heat until the wine is nearly evaporated. Add the remaining wine and chicken stock. Stir in the Wondra until slightly thickened, add the tarragon.

Return the chicken to the pan, baste and cover. Cook over a low heat for 30 minutes, then remove the chicken.

Add the rest of the butter and cream. If not thick enough add a little more Wondra. Heat, salt and pepper to taste, pour over the chicken and serve.

★ ☆ ★

Blythe Danner
BLYTHE'S CHICKEN
serves 4

1 frying chicken (3 lbs), cut into pieces
6 Tbs butter
2 Tbs vegetable oil
16-24 whole shallots
salt and pepper
2 bay leaves
1 Tbs chopped parsley
11/2 tsp lemon juice
frozen artichoke hearts, defrosted and drained
1/2 cup chicken stock

In a large skillet, brown the chicken, skin side down, in 4 Tbs of butter and the 2 Tbs of oil until golden. Remove and set aside. Peel the shallots and, in the same pan, sauté them until golden. Drain off most of the fat; return the chicken to the pan; season with salt and pepper; place the bay leaves on top; sprinkle with parsley; cover and cook on a low flame for 30 minutes. Baste occasionally.

In a saucepan, melt the remaining 2 Tbs butter. Add the lemon juice and the drained artichoke hearts. Cover and cook over a low flame until the artichokes are tender (about 15 minutes).

Arrange the chicken pieces on a platter and decorate the plate with the shallots and artichokes. Discard the bay leaves.

Deglaze the pan with the chicken stock over high heat. Reduce the sauce to 1/2 cup, pour over the chicken. Serve immediately.

★ ☆ ★

This recipe along with the Holiday Jello Mold (pg.196) are from my mom, Dorothy J. Taylor, a great pianist, painter and mother of six daughters who are all in the theatre. To my son, Shaun, she is Grandma Dorothy and he has been known to present her with "Certificates of Good Cooking" and other awards such as dried-up cicada skins.

-Lynne Taylor-Corbett

CHICKEN BREASTS a la D. J. TAYLOR
serves 6

6-8 thinly sliced chicken breasts
2 cups seasoned bread crumbs or cubes
1 egg, well beaten
2-4 Tbs chicken broth
1 onion, finely chopped
1/2 cup slivered almonds
1/2 cup diced black olives
1 Tbs sage
salt and pepper
toothpicks
3 Tbs butter, melted
fresh parsley and lemon slices for garnish

In a large bowl, moisten bread crumbs with the egg. Add the chicken broth slowly so that the consistancy does not become mushy. Sauté the onions in a bit of oil or butter and add to the wet bread crumbs. Stir in the slivered almonds and the olives. Season with sage, salt and pepper. Allow to sit for 15 minutes.

Wash and pat dry the chicken breasts. Put a portion of the dressing onto each piece and roll tightly; secure the rolled pieces with a toothpick or two. Brush with melted butter and place in a lightly oiled, covered baking dish. Bake for 15 minutes in a 350° oven, remove the lid and continue to bake for 6-10 minutes or until brown. Remove toothpicks. Serve on a bed of parsley and garnish with lemon slices.

My husband, Robert Emmett, is a writer; my son, Sean, a musician who lives and works in Las Vegas; and my daughter, Kathryn, an attorney in Stamford, Connecticut. This recipe was developed in honor of our son, Sean Emmett - Cape Scott, Vancouver Island. This was where his devotion to brown rice first saw light of day. As I recall, it was the Summer of 1972.

-Kim Hunter

CAPE SCOTT CHICKEN
serves 4-6

1 (3 lb) chicken, cut into 8-10 pieces
garlic salt
fresh ground black pepper
paprika
3 cups chicken stock
1 tsp salt
1/2 tsp saffron (optional)
1 cup brown rice
1 lb carrots, scraped and cut in 1-inch slices
2 or 3 medium onions, peeled and cut into 8 wedges each
2 Tbs parsley, finely chopped
3 Tbs raisins (optional)
1/2 lb fresh green peas

Wash and dry the chicken pieces; cut away any excess fat. Sprinkle liberally with garlic salt, pepper and paprika. Place the chicken pieces, skin side up, in a shallow baking pan large enough for them to lie in one layer without touching. Bake 10 to 15 minutes in the hottest oven - 550°, preheated. When they're brown and crispy and well-rendered of fat, remove the pieces from the pan to paper toweling to drain.

Bring the chicken stock to a boil in a casserole that is large enough to hold the chicken in one layer. Add the salt, a bit more pepper, saffron and rice. Stir well. Mix in the carrots, onions, parsley and raisins. Place the chicken on top, skin side up. Do not overlap.

Cover the casserole and bake in a preheated 325° oven for 1 hour. Remove the casserole from the oven, lift the chicken out, and scatter the peas over the vegetables. Put the chicken back on top, cover the dish and continue to bake for 1/2 hour. Serve immediately.

This chicken recipe is the first thing I ever cooked, I think! I was a student at Boston University and had invited a bunch over to my new, and first, apartment. In a panic, I called home asking my mother what the hell I was supposed to do now. She sent this recipe with her usual words of encouragement. It all went fine.

Years later, when I was starring in La Cage *on Broadway, Macy's Department Store asked me to come out to their Queens kitchen and cook something for a publicity thing. I remembered this dish but had long since lost it. Again, Mom came to the rescue. She poured through all the old card files until she found it and bailed me out of Queens, where it was just as successful as in my Boston apartment.*

-Walter Charles

COUNTRY CAPTAIN CHICKEN
serves 6-8 (and looks good, too)

2 lbs boneless chicken breasts
seasoned flour
1/2 cup shortening
2 onions, finely chopped
2 green peppers, chopped
1 clove garlic, minced
1/2 tsp thyme
3-4 tsp curry powder
11/2 tsp salt
1/2 tsp white pepper
2 cans whole, seedless tomatoes (1 lb, 3 oz each)
1 Tbs chopped parsley
6 cups cooked rice, kept hot
1/4 cup currants
1/4 lb toasted almonds
parsley sprigs for garnish

Remove skin from the chicken, roll breasts in the seasoned flour and fry in shortening until browned. Remove chicken from pan and keep warm in the oven. In the same fry pan, cook the onions, peppers and garlic, on a low flame, until tender but not browned. Stir in the thyme, curry powder, salt and pepper; mix well. Add the tomatoes and chopped parsley, continue to cook until well heated.

Place the chicken in a large casserole dish and pour the sauce over the breasts. Cover and bake at 350° for 45 minutes.

Arrange the chicken in the center of a large serving platter, mound the cooked rice around the breasts. Add the currants to the sauce and pour over the rice. Sprinkle the almonds over the chicken, garnish and serve.

★ ☆ ★

This dish is for the last minute dinner invite and your ingredients should be on hand. That's the fun of it!

-Sylvia Miles

MY FAST CHICKEN
serves 2

The only requirements are:

frozen chicken parts (6 pieces)
1 can button mushrooms, in butter sauce
1 can tinned onion flakes
some left-over wine
25 minutes

Don't defrost the chicken parts.

Get a big pan and put in the chicken, onion flakes, the mushrooms, along with their sauce, and some wine.

Cover and simmer for about 25 minutes. Add salt and pepper to taste.

The juices will simmer and sizzle to a delightful wine sauce.

I like to use BUNCHES of garlic! Serve with rice or noodles, either is great. ENJOY!
-Nell Carter

NELL CARTER'S FAVORITE CHICKEN
serves 4

1 whole chicken, cut up
1 lb mushrooms
4 tomatoes
6 scallions
2 garlic cloves
1 red onion
1 yellow onion
salt and pepper
1 Tbs margarine
3 Tbs vegetable oil
Parmesan cheese

Chop the mushrooms, tomatoes, scallions, garlic,and onions and sauté in margarine. Season the vegetables only from the top. While they are sautéing, heat the oil in a shallow pan and cook the chicken, uncovered, for approximately 25 minutes. Pour the sautéed mixture over the cooked chicken, cover and continue to cook for 20 more minutes. Sprinkle with Parmesan cheese (a lot if you like) and cook 10 minutes more. Remove and EAT!

My husband, whom I love more than anything in the world, did not quite figure out that when he got me I wasn't exactly going to be Susie Homemaker - in the kitchen at least. Now, since he grew up in the south and I love fried chicken, I figured I'd make us both happy. It all came together magically when his very southern aunt gave me this recipe for Christmas. Thank you Aunt Ginnie.

-Debbie Shapiro

BUTTERMILK FRIED CHICKEN
serves 4-6

2 cups all purpose flour
1 Tbs salt
1 tsp paprika
1/2 tsp pepper
1 cup buttermilk
1 tsp baking powder
3 lbs chicken, in pieces
oil (I always use olive oil. It makes me feel my fried chicken is healthy to eat.)

Combine the first four ingredients in a plastic or paper bag; shake to mix and set aside.

Combine buttermilk and baking powder in a bowl. Mix well.

Dip chicken a piece at a time in the buttermilk mixture. Place chicken in the bag and shake. Repeat with each piece. Place the chicken in a shallow pan, cover and refrigerate at least 1 hour. (The longer the better.)

Heat 1 inch of non-fattening healthy oil in a large skillet to 325°. Add the chicken and fry 30-35 minutes or until golden brown. Turn only once. Drain and serve and *save some for me.*

What to do with left-over chicken, turkey or lamb? The following recipe is unique in using left-over lamb whose flavor is not normally enhanced by recooking. The name of the dish is Nasi Goring. It is a staple of Balinese cooking and translated literally from Malaysian is "fried rice" ...or rather "rice fried."

-Al Hirschfeld

NASI GORING
serves 4-6

2 cups Uncle Ben's rice, cooked
1/4 lb butter, margarine or peanut oil
3 large onions, diced
3 stalks celery, diced
3 garlic cloves, thinly sliced
cayenne pepper
1 to 2 lbs cooked chicken, turkey or lamb
2 cups chicken soup (consommé or stock)
2 eggs, well beaten
1 tsp salt
Tabasco sauce
soy sauce
chutney and Japanese Rice Crackers

Melt butter in large skillet, add onion, celery and garlic. Sauté lightly. Sprinkle with cayenne pepper and a teaspoon of salt. Add bite-sized pieces of chicken, turkey or lamb. Lower the flame and stir in the soup, eggs and the cooked rice. Stir constantly for about 20 minutes, add 8 drops of Tabasco and soy sauce to taste. Serve with chutney and rice crackers.

For more festive occasions, this dish may be elaboratley decorated with fried bananas and fried apple slices and sprinkled generously with unsweetened grated coconut, raisins and unsalted peanuts.

★ ☆ ★

This is the quickest chicken dinner in the world and aptly named.

-Phyllis Newman

QUICKEST CHICKEN DINNER IN THE WORLD
serves 4

2 chickens cut-up
soy sauce (enough to cover chicken)
lemon juice and fresh pepper to taste
4 Tbs honey

Create a marinade by mixing the liquid ingredients. Pour over chicken and place in refrigerator as along as you can.

Place in baking pan and broil for one hour, turning and basting occasionally. Take out when brown and crispy on top.

This one recipe can last all week. It's great during rehearsals when time is scarce. Have fun with it!

-Ann Reinking

REINKING'S CHICKEN AND DUMPLINGS
serves 2-4

1 whole chicken, quartered
1/2 gallon chicken broth
1/2 cup peas
3 carrots, scrubbed and sliced
1 chicken bouillon cube
thyme
rosemary
bay leaves
1 medium onion, minced
1 clove garlic, minced
Bisquick
country sausage
salt and pepper

Put the chicken, broth, peas, carrots, bouillon and spices in a large pot. Be exceptionally liberal with the herbs. Place on a low to medium flame and allow to simmer.

Prepare dumplings according to the Bisquick package directions.

In a skillet, brown the sausage.

Add the dumplings and the sausage to the pot. Let simmer until the sauce thickens. If the liquid evaporates too quickly, add a little water and another bouillon cube.

I can't take full credit for this recipe; however, I came upon it on the road in 1975 while I was doing Purlie. *I credit my dear friend Freda Vanterpool-Morris with this guaranteed fun food.*

-Ken Page

CHICKEN ON THE ROAD
serves 2

1 whole chicken, cut up
1 paper bag, to shake the chicken in (be sure not to eat it)
flour
1 tsp garlic salt
1 tsp cumin
1 tsp pepper
1/2 tsp salt
1 cup milk
1 egg, well beaten
honey

Fill the bag half way with flour, add the spices.

In a bowl, mix the milk and egg. Dip the chicken in the mixture (it feels awful but hang in there). Put the chicken pieces in the bag (remember that) and shake (while Patti LaBelle's "Lady Marmalade" plays on the CD circa 1975).

Fry the chicken any way you like. After it is wonderfully crispy remove from the pan and drain on paper toweling. Sprinkle a little extra cumin on the chicken and then... this is the great part... pour honey over the chicken while it's hot.

Now you must invite all your friends over and turn up "Lady Marmalade" and enjoy! *Thanks Freda.*

From the Editor:

    Mr. Walken tells me this simple, but wonderful, recipe is of his own creation but will never divulge its true beginnings.

Christopher Walken
ROASTED TARRAGON CHICKEN
serves 4-6

a fresh chicken
garlic, crushed
1 lemon
salt, pepper and tarragon to taste

Put a cut lemon inside the chicken with some fresh garlic. Outside, sprinkle with salt, pepper and tarragon to taste. Bake hot 'til crispy/done. (350° oven, about 20 minutes per pound. -Ed.)

Serving suggestions: A simple oil and vinegar salad. Bagel crisps. Steamed asparagus flavored with oregano and butter. A chilled, Italian crispy white wine. Some great cookies for dessert, with Espresso and Brandy.

This dish is in honor of actress Vicki Lewis, whom I love.

-Lewis J. Stadlin

CHICKEN a la VICKI
serves 2-4

1 whole roasting or frying chicken
4 baby potatoes
4 baby onions
1/2 Spanish onion
3 carrots, cut in pieces vertically 1" long
1 lemon
2 Tbs soy sauce
1/4 cup white cooking wine
8 cloves garlic, minced
5 fingers basil
5 fingers of tarragon
garlic powder

Preheat oven to 350°.

Wash and dry chicken. With fingers, gently separate the skin of the chicken from the meat and spoon several heaping portions of the minced garlic along the breast and bottom side of the bird beneath the skin. Use the remaining garlic to coat the outside of the bird.

Place the chicken into a Dutch Oven along with your potatoes, baby onions and carrots. Pour 1/4 cup of water into the pot and pour your cooking wine over the chicken. Sprinkle the basil and tarragon all over the chicken along with the soy sauce. Cut a lemon in half and squeeze its contents all over the skin. Then place it inside the chicken along with the Spanish onion. Liberally sprinkle the bird with garlic powder. Cover the Dutch Oven and cook for 11/2 hours. Remove at least twice and baste it with its own juices. After 11/2 hours remove the lid and cook for another 1/2 hour. Divide the bird in half. Serve with the carrots, onions and potatoes. Pour the juices over the chicken.

Serve with white wine and a tomato and onion salad. Your woman will love you and she may even do the dishes.

Meats

Beef Curry
Hamburger Curry a la Sylvia Miles
Brenda's Meatloaf
Yankee Meatloaf
Sauerbraten
Szekelyi Gulyas
Mediterranean Stew
Yam Nua
Glazed Hamloaf
Kasha Pork Casserole
Kielbasa and Sauerkraut
Garrett-Parks Lamb Curry
Juliet Prowse's Lamb Curry
Leg of Lamb Almost as Good-Lookin' as Mine
Loubia

The first time Pat cooked for me I asked for a soft boiled egg. (This was in the evening, lest you get the wrong impression!) She hadn't cooked much for a number of years and had absolutely no idea how long the egg should boil. Thirty minutes later I was served what could have easily passed for a rubber ball and she watched as I bravely attempted to chase it around the plate. I'm sure I heard "BOING" at each stab. When I finally managed to take a bite the exchange went like this: "Yuck! Yuck!" "What's the matter?" she said, all wide-eyed and innocent. "Oh, nothing," I replied. "It's just that one hopes when one meets a woman that she knows how to cook!"

-John Simon

Since then I've managed to find my way around the kitchen and, yes, I can make soft boiled eggs! This Beef Curry is a festive dish for entertaining because each guest can decorate his plate with the colorful garnishes. I served it one night for an after theatre supper and was cornered in the kitchen by an actor who proclaimed, "John's accent has to be fake. No one could have lived in this country all these years and still sound like that!" (Which is to say a Transylvanian Charles Boyer.) I've since heard the same theory from a number of people. Say what you will about John; let me assure you - everything (including the accent) is real.

This Curry is nice served with breadsticks and raw vegetables and a favorite of John's with a Sacher Torte (pg. 201) for dessert.

-Patricia Hoag

BEEF CURRY
serves 10-12

3 lbs beef stew cubes
2 Tbs olive oil
2 medium onions, chopped
2 large cloves garlic, crushed
2 cups peeled and grated green apple
4 Tbs curry powder
2 cans condensed beef broth, undiluted
1 cup raisins
2 tsp salt
chutney
cooked rice, hot
Assorted condiments: coconut, mandarin orange slices,
        cucumber, onion, chopped peanuts

In a large kettle, brown the beef in hot oil. Add the onions and garlic. Cook for about five minutes, stirring, until the onions are tender. Stir in the apples and curry and continue to cook about three minutes. Add the beef broth, raisins, salt and 1/4 cup chutney. Bring the mixture to a boil, cover and simmer for 2 hours or until the beef is tender. Stir occasionally. Serve on a bed rice with the condiments of your choice.

I created this delicious Hamburger Curry, but I did accept a little suggestion of the raisins and coconut from Jean Dalrymple, the estimable producer and gourmet cook.

-Sylvia Miles

HAMBURGER CURRY a la SYLVIA MILES
serves 4

1 apple, peeled, cored and chopped
2 medium onions, finely chopped
1 clove garlic, minced
1 Tbs peanut oil
1 lb ground chuck
2 Tbs curry powder
1 tsp salt
2 stalks celery, chopped
1/2 cup raisins
1 can beef gravy
1 small can tomato sauce
3 Tbs unsweetened, grated coconut

Sauté apple, onions and garlic in oil for 5 minutes. Add the ground chuck, break it up with a fork and brown gently. Sprinkle with curry powder and salt. Then add the celery, raisins, gravy, tomato sauce and coconut. Stir well and cover. Simmer over a low heat for about an hour, stirring occasionally. Serve with rice, mango chutney and any of the various condiments usually served with Indian cuisine.

Brenda Vaccaro
BRENDA'S MEATLOAF
serves 2-4

11/2 lbs ground beef
1 can condensed, creamed chicken or mushroom soup
3/4 cup seasoned bread crumbs
1/4 cup parsley, basil and chives, chopped
salt and pepper
10 or more Spanish olives, chopped
OR water chestnuts
1 8oz can tomato sauce

Mix all ingredients in a large bowl. Place in a 4" X 8" X 4" glass baking dish. Bake for 45 minutes in a 350° oven.

After the loaf has cooked for about one half hour add the tomato sauce, a little dried basil and oregano and finish cooking. Let loaf stand 10 minutes before slicing and serve with the sauce.

I owe the creation of my favorite meatloaf and my favorite dessert (see pg. 187) recipes to my two dear friends: Stephen Bernstein and Danny Cass. I am happy to share them with you as they did with me.

-Robert Morse

YANKEE MEATLOAF
serves 8

1 lb ground beef
1 lb ground veal or pork
11/2 cups milk
11/2 cups seasoned bread crumbs
2 onions, chopped and sautéed in olive oil
1 red pepper, chopped and sautéed in olive oil
2 eggs
1 Tbs Dijon mustard

1 tsp chopped basil
1 tsp dried thyme
1 tsp rosemary
1 tsp fresh ground black pepper

Combine all ingredients in a large bowl and mix well. Form into a loaf and place into a baking pan.

Bake at 325° for 35 minutes, then cover the meatloaf with the following mushroom mixture and bake for another 10 to 15 minutes. Remove from oven and let stand 15 minutes before serving.

Mushroom Mixture
11/2 lbs mushrooms
4 Tbs butter
2 Tbs olive oil
2 cloves crushed garlic
1/4 cup apple cider

Slice the mushrooms and sauté in the butter, olive oil and garlic, until tender. Spread the sautéed mushrooms over the meatloaf. Deglaze the pan with the apple cider allowing it to reduce by half, pour over the mushrooms.

If you've never tasted Sauerbraten, I'll make a flat claim that you haven't lived until you've tasted mine. The work time is short, the marinating time long. While the meat is resting in the marinade it must remain cool in order not to spoil. If there's not enough room for it in your refrigerator, wait until the outside temperature is between 40° and 60° to store the marinating meat on a fire escape in the city or a tool room or cool basement in the country.

-Uta Hagen

SAUERBRATEN
serves 6-8

5 lbs of eye-round of beef, rolled and tied by the butcher

If you've heard that it must be larded, rest assured. I don't have it done.

Place the meat in a glass, enamel or porcelain bowl that will hold it snugly and surround with the following ingredients:

2 onions, sliced
2 leeks, sliced (white parts only)
2 carrots, sliced
1 turnip, sliced
6 whole cloves
12 peppercorns
12 crushed juniper berries*

*Don't eliminate the juniper berries because they *make* the Sauerbraten. They're available in the spice department of any good grocery store.

Sprinkle everything with 2 tsp coarse salt, and pour on 1 qt boiling red wine vinegar. Cover the dish with plastic wrap, then with a lid and keep cool for one week. Turn the meat in the marinade once a day.

On the day of your party, take the meat from the marinade and drain in a colander for 1/2 hour. Then dry it thoroughly with toweling so it will brown well. Put the marinade into a heavy pot, large enough to hold the meat, and set it over a very low flame.

Meanwhile, brown the meat evenly on all sides in a large skillet in: 2 Tbs fat (goose fat is ideal; bacon fat will do). The browning should take about 15 minutes. Regulate the heat so the fat won't burn. Remove the meat and arrange it among the vegetables in the hot marinade. Cover tightly and simmer for 21/2 hours, turning the meat over once after an hour or so. Pierce to see if it is tender. It may need as much as another 30 minutes of simmering. When done, remove it carefully from the pot and cut off the strings. Keep it hot on a platter in a 200° oven while you make the sauce.

For The Sauce
To the marinade in the pot add 1 cup dry red wine. Boil it down for at least 5 minutes and strain through a sieve, pressing down hard on the vegetables to extract the flavor. Let rest for a few minutes before skimming off all possible fat.

In a skillet melt 1 stick of butter (8 Tbs). Add 4 Tbs quick-mix flour. Over low heat, blend and cook for a few minutes. Add 2 Tbs sugar and the strained marinade. Cook and stir until the sauce thickens. Serve it at the table in a pitcher.

My wife, Karel Shimoff, learned to make this recipe from Hungarian-born Elsa Nikolic. Elsa is a dress designer, sculptress, painter and friend whom I met in New York, through my wife, while doing a Broadway show.

Once, I was doing a film in England and had some time off and I wanted to see Paris - my first time; I was 19. I asked my friends what I should see and where I should go. A must on everybody's list was dinner at the famous Tour d'Argent overlooking all of Paris. The second night of my stay in Paris, I went. The Maitre d' was in tails, the waiters wore tails and white gloves. Everyone was dressed to the teeth.

After a very expensive main course - I can't remember what, but something very French and exotic (not Szekeli Gulyas) - the waiter brought me a large platter with a soup plate on top holding three white, steaming, tightly wrapped, what looked to me like crepes. I thought, "This probably goes with the meal, something I haven't ordered." I wasn't sure what I had ordered! The waiter brought no silver which I thought was odd. I picked up one of the crepes, bit down and started to chew. My taste buds recognized the familiar texture of a wash cloth; I was trying to eat a finger towel. I felt every elegant eye in the Tour d'Argent upon me. With a sickly smile I nonchalantly wiped my fingers and as the waiter cleared his throat and asked if I'd like dessert. I said, "No, I think I've had enough, Merci."

-Tommy Rall

SZEKELYI GULYAS
serves 4

2 lbs sauerkraut
1 to 2 cups beef broth or cubes
2 lbs lean stew meat
2 Tbs oil to brown meat
1 large onion, chopped
1 tsp paprika
salt to taste
1 pkg cocktail franks
1 pint sour cream

Strain and squeeze sauerkraut, wash and squeeze again. Put sauerkraut in a large pot along with 1 or 2 cups broth (enough to cook but not swim). Cook slowly; with the cover off center.

Brown meat in oil and remove from pan. Sauté the chopped onion in that pan until tender and drain off fat. Return meat to the pan and add 1 tsp salt, cover tightly, simmer until juices begin to form. Then add the paprika, and a little water if the mixture seems dry. Let it stew slowly for 1/2 hour. In a greased casserole, layer the sauerkraut and meat with the franks alternately, ending with a layer of sauerkraut. Cook tightly covered at 300° for 1 hour. Serve with sour cream and steamed rice or boiled potatoes, Bulls Blood wine and seltzer.

Do not attempt to perform on any stage for at least 48 hours after this meal.

Ed Asner's
MEDITERRANEAN STEW
serves 6-8

1 lb chuck steak, cut into 11/2" cubes
1 lb sweet Italian sausage
11/2 cups burgundy wine
2 cups water
1 6oz can tomato paste
3/4 tsp pepper
3 minced garlic cloves
2 tsp paprika
1 lb cooked ham
3 medium onions, coarsley chopped
1 sweet red pepper, coarsley chopped
1/4 cup chopped fresh parsley
2 1 lb cans garbanzo beans, drained
1 tsp grated lemon rind
1 head cabbage

In a skillet, sauté beef cubes and sausage until brown. Drain meats and slice sausage; transfer to Dutch Oven. Add wine, water, tomato paste, salt, pepper, garlic and paprika. Bring to a boil, cover and simmer 11/2 to 2 hours or until meat is tender.

Add remaining ingredients except cabbage. Cover and cook about 20 minutes; add cabbage and cook until crisp-tender, about 15-20 minutes. Refrigerate overnight to develop flavors. Skim off fat. Bring stew to room temperature. Reheat in microwave oven 4-5 minutes; top of range 15-20 minutes or until hot.

I fell in love with my Thai cooking teacher long before we ever actually met. I was a teenage dancer in summer stock and she was a serene goddess, in a towering headdress, in an old poster on a Cape Cod pizzeria wall. The poster read "Beautiful Thailand" and I agreed.

In 1970, on West 79th Street in N.Y.C., the first Thai restaurant in the United States opened its doors. I was there ... and so was she. She owned it!!

Lady "Nancy" Maharakkaka had been the prima ballerina at the Royal Thai Court when her image had lured thousands to "Beautiful Thailand." She became my friend and teacher in all things Thai. As her Aunt was in charge of the Royal Kitchens at the Grand Palace in Bangkok, Nancy learned her cooking skills from the very best, and since I learned from Nancy, so did I.

Nancy Maharakkaka is prominent and popular among the Thai community here. It is no surprise! After all, how many gals can carve veggies into flowers that look real, prepare a dinner fit for a King, then throw on a crown and be the floor show?!

-Arthur Faria

YAM NUA (Thai Beef Salad)
serves 2-4

1 lb beef sirloin
1 medium red onion, sliced in thin rounds and halved
juice of 1 large lime
2 Tbs nam pla (fish sauce)*
2 tsp sugar
5 cloves garlic, finely chopped
1/2 cup fresh mint leaves, chopped
2 dried red chilies, ground
1 head red leaf lettuce
1 cucumber, sliced in thin rounds
1 dozen cherry tomatoes, cut in half
1 bunch pak chee (cilantro, Chinese parsley)*

Roast the beef on a barbecue or under the broiler until rare. Let cool and slice into 3 inch long strips.

Mix together lime juice, nam pla, sugar, garlic, mint and dried chilies and set aside.

In a separate bowl, toss together the beef and red onion. Add the lime juice/chili mixture, mix with your hands and refrigerate until ready to serve.

Cover a serving platter with the lettuce leaves. Arrange the cucumber rounds on the perimeter of the lettuce and place a tomato half on each round. Mound the salad in the center of the platter and decorate with pak chee leaves.

* These ingredients are available at any Oriental market or Gourmet shop.

This dish, which was given to me by my mother, Mrs. Donald F. Elliott, has been served at many cast parties. It makes an excellent late supper and is particularly good for entertaining because it can be completely prepared ahead of time and warmed up just before serving. It also freezes very well.

I especially like this recipe because it reminds me of my parent's elegant buffet supper parties in Indiana.

-Kenneth Elliott

GLAZED HAMLOAF

For The Meatloaf
2 lbs lean smoked ham, ground
2 lbs lean fresh pork, ground
11/2 cups cracker crumbs
1/3 cup chopped onion
4 eggs, well beaten
2 cups milk
2 Tbs chopped parsley

For The Glaze
1/2 cup brown sugar
1/2 cup vinegar
11/2 Tbs dry mustard

For The Sauce
1 pint sour cream
1 Tbs horseradish

Combine all the meatloaf ingredients and shape into 2 loaves. Place each in a 9"
X 5" X 3" loaf pan. Bake for 30 minutes in a 350° oven.

Combine the glaze ingredients and pour over the loaves and bake for 1 hour more. Let the loaves sit for 15 minutes before serving.

Mix the sour cream (some prefer whipped cream) with the horseradish and serve along with the loaves.

Walter Matthau
KASHA PORK CASSEROLE

Take one cup of buckwheat groats and mix in 2 eggs. Put mixture in a very hot skillet or frying pan and scramble groats with a fork. Pour 2 1/2 cups of chicken broth into the separated groats and simmer for 15 minutes. Mix in 1/2 a minced onion or scallions and cubed pieces of pork, pork sausage or chicken breast; or whatever meat or cheese products you like.

This is my favorite recipe.

Both this recipe and The World's Best Potato Salad (pg. 175) are two of the dishes that were served at my grandmother's house in Bayonne, N.J. She was the head of the Russian household in my Irish/Russian upbringing. Her eight children and their husbands and or wives and their children would gather for the Russian holidays, Easter and "Little" Christmas. While my grandfather was alive, he used to stuff and smoke his own blend of keilbasa behind a wood-burning stove.

Other dishes served were stuffed cabbage (Ha-Lup-Key); perogies, small pies stuffed with potato, sauerkraut or prunes; and a large assortment of cookies and pastries. These days I celebrate Christmas Eve with my parents and sisters in Pennsylvania, but I return to the city for Christmas Day dinner with friends and neighbors. We all bring different dishes. I always bring Keilbasa and Sauerkraut and Potato Salad.

While cooking these dishes in my apartment, the aromas remind me of those festive occasions at my Grandmother's and the memory of a terrific lady and wonderful cook.

-Ray Gill

KIELBASA AND SAUERKRAUT
serves 4

1 ring of good quality kielbasa (pronounced Koo-Bah-See), about 1 1/2 lbs
1 1 lb package sauerkraut
1 large onion, chopped
1 tsp butter

Boil the keilbasa for 10 minutes.

Melt the butter in a large skillet and brown the onion.

Drain the sauerkraut and stir into the skillet. Stir for three minutes. Remove the keilbasa from the boiling water and cut into 1 inch pieces. Add to the skillet, turn and serve.

★ ☆ ★

One of the favorite meals in our family (which consisted of Larry Parks, my husband; our two sons, Garrett and Andrew; and my mother, Octavia Garrett) was Lamb Curry. However, Lamb Curry usually came after having leg of lamb. The lamb was cooked with a lot of rosemary, thyme and marjoram. That would be dinner one night. I would roast a chicken the second night and on the third I would chop up all the leftover lamb and leftover chicken and that was the basis of the Garrett-Parks Lamb Curry. So I suspect some of the spices that the lamb and chicken were cooked with sneaked into the curry making it quite special. Larry was a great one for bringing interesting facts to the dinner table. His research on curry revealed that when curry was served to the British Colonists in India, a separate Indian servant brought on each relish to be eaten with the curry. Thus, if there were 10 small bowls of the different relishes, it was referred to as "10 boy curry." So this recipe is "10 boy curry" without the 10 boys. We served ours on a large lazy susan in the center of the table and this made it extra fun for my boys.

-Betty Garrett

GARRETT-PARKS LAMB CURRY
serves 4

1 lb lamb shoulder, cut into cubes
3 Tbs fat
1 cup boiling water

1/2 tsp salt
1/4 tsp pepper
2/3 tsp curry powder (I like more. If you like it hot add more.)
1 Tbs chopped onion
1/4 cup or more chopped celery
1 Tbs chopped pimento
1 Tbs chopped parsley

In a large skillet, heat the fat and brown the meat. Add all the remaining ingredients, cover and simmer for 20 to 30 minutes. Stir frequently. Thicken stock with flour. Stir for two minutes. When using leftovers, allow to cook until flavor is cooked through. It may take a little longer.

Serve with 10 small bowls containing one of each of the following:

raisins
chives
nuts
cubed, fresh tomatoes
coconut
cubed, fresh cucumber
chopped hard boiled egg white
Major Grey's Chutney
chopped hard boiled egg yolk
rice (naturally, a large bowl is required)

Serve the curry over rice and a sprinkle from each bowl adds all kinds of tastes and textures.

★ ☆ ★

My first New York audition, and subsequent job, was for Juliet Prowse in her nightclub act. Juliet introduced me to a lot of firsts; however, I'm only going to tell you about her Curry.

Being from Covington, Kentucky I didn't even know what curry was. Juliet is from Johannesburg, South Africa and her East Indian/British influence resulted in this recipe.

There were many nights in Las Vegas when we would sit down with this treat and a bottle of Champagne after the show. It won't guarantee long beautiful legs like Juliet's, but it sure was wonderful watching her stand on hers as she cooked this curry.

-Lee Roy Reams

JULIET PROWSE'S LAMB CURRY
serves 4-6

2 sticks butter
2 medium onions, chopped
4 cloves, chopped
1 stick cinnamon
2 Tbs curry powder
1/4 lb lamb per person (chicken can also be used)
4 large ripe tomatoes (or canned equivalent), sliced
raisins, shredded coconut and chutney as relishes

On a low flame, melt butter and add chopped onion, garlic and cinnamon. Cook until golden. Add the curry powder and let cook for 2 minutes before you add the tomatoes. Cover the pan and cook until mushy. Stir in the lamb. Simmer for two hours on a low flame. Serve with wild rice. Put the raisins, coconut and chutney in decorative bowls and serve on the side.

★ ☆ ★

Alyson Reed
LEG OF LAMB
ALMOST AS GOOD-LOOKIN' AS MINE
serves 4-6

1 leg of lamb
2 cloves of garlic, silced
anchovies, just a few for flavor
11/2 Tbs Dijon mustard
11/2 Tbs light oil
rosemary leaves

Pre-heat oven to 375°. For those *Psycho*-holics, take a butcher knife and stab the leg of lamb a few times. Stud the lamb with the garlic slices and anchovies. Put a *Blob* of Dijon in a cup and slowly whip in the light oil. Slowly is important. It should be a frothy pudding mixture. Scoop your hand into the mustard/oil mixture and spread all over the leg of lamb. Coat both sides with rosemary leaves. Place in the oven for 11/2 hours or until you like the shade.

Be sure to wash your hands before greeting your guests!

This is a recipe from my father-in-law's cookbook. His name was Armand Coullet. He died at age 85 only weeks after the book was published. He insisted he had to "stay alive to finish my book." And he did! He was quite a guy and I have enjoyed many of the recipes from his book, especially the French-Algerian ones. He was born and raised there.

-Anita Gillette

LOUBIA
serves 6

11/2 lbs lamb (leg or shoulder), diced
1 lb dry white Navy beans
2 onions, chopped

3 cloves garlic, chopped
1 sprig parsley
3 ripe tomatoes, peeled
1 Tbs flour
1 tsp thyme
4 bay leaves
1 tsp oregano
2 tsp paprika
8 cloves
dask of hot cayenne pepper (optional)

Allow beans to soak overnight, then cook in cold water (no salt).

In a deep iron pot put 2 Tbs olive oil. When oil is hot, brown meat over very low fire. Add onions. When onions are golden brown, add tomatoes. When tomatoes are well integrated, stir in flour. Then, add 3 cups of very hot water and season with thyme, bay leaves, oregano, paprika, cloves, salt and pepper.

When meat is done, add beans. Stir and cook another 15 minutes. Then, add garlic and parsley chopped fine together and cook an additional 15 minutes. Remove bay leaves. Serve hot.

My father-in-law noted in his book that the Loubia is a favorite Algerian dish. It is a mainstay to the natives but often unsuspecting tourists would wander into a "Gargotte," or restaurant catering to the local trade, and order this unusual, substantial dish giving them a true feeling for North African cooking.

★ ☆ ★

Vegetable Dishes

Egyptian Bean Salad
Gerry's Baked Beans
Champ
Spinach Tofu Lasagna
Potato Pancakes
Diller's Deli Potato Salad
The World's Best Potato Salad
Very Satisfying Baked Potato Skins
Stuft Spuds
Stir Fry Spinach
Spaghetti Squash Pasta
Puréed Vegetables
Steamed Herbed Vegetables
Zucchini Parmesan
Stuffed Zucchini

I was introduced to Foul (pronounced: fool), or Egyptian Bean Salad, late one night after a show (Modigliani) by Ethan Phillips. It is totally irresistible and you can safely offer $5.00 to anyone who can take just one mouthful and then stop.

-Jeffrey DeMunn

EGYPTIAN BEAN SALAD

1 can Fava Beans (or your favorite), drained
1/2 bulb garlic, finely chopped
juice of 2 lemons
1/4 cup olive oil
salt and pepper
1 large bunch parsley, finely chopped
2 tomatoes, chopped

Put the beans, garlic, lemon juice, oil, salt and pepper in a sauce pan. Bring nearly to a boil, add chopped parsley and chill. Stir in the chopped tomatoes just before serving.

OR - Add the tomatoes right away and serve warm.

Gerry Longo is my dearest friend in the world! She also happens to be one of the greatest cooks I know. (Being a "tenor" I need to be fed in the grand style.) One Thanksgiving, Gerry had outdone herself by preparing enough food for an army. (She knew I'd be there.) To her dismay and delight, I tasted the baked beans first and spent a fabulous Thanksgiving stuffing myself into "Baked Bean Heaven."

P.S. I really think what makes Gerry's food taste extra special is the love she adds to all her recipes.

-David Romano

GERRY'S BAKED BEANS
serves a lot of people

2 cans (16 oz each) Campbell's Old Fashioned Baked Beans
2 cans Campbell's Home Style Baked Beans
2 cans Campbell's Pork and Beans
3 large onions, sliced
1/2 lb uncooked bacon, sliced
fresh ground black pepper

For The Sauce
In a large bowl mix:
6oz tomato ketchup
8oz barbecue sauce
1/2 cup dark Karo Syrup
4oz Heinz Chili Sauce
1/2 cup brown sugar
dash of Worchester Sauce
onion salt
garlic salt

Layer 1/3 can of each kind of bean in a large, oven-safe pot. Next, layer a thin covering of onions and then bacon. Spoon sauce over and sprinkle with black pepper. Repeat, in layers, until all the ingredients are used up.

Bake covered in a 375° oven for 5 to 6 hours.

Jeremy Irons
CHAMP
serves 4

11/2 lbs freshly cooked mashed potatoes
4 Tbs melted butter
salt and pepper
10 spring onions
OR 2 leeks cooked in 1/2 cup milk

Cook the chopped spring onions, green part as well as white, in the milk. Drain and keep the milk. Mash the potatoes, season to taste and add the spring onions. Beat well together and add enough hot milk to make the dish creamy and smooth.

Place mixture in a deep, warmed dish making a well in the center and pour the hot, melted butter into well. The dry potato should be dipped in the pool of butter when serving.

CHAMP can also be made with chopped parsley, chives, young nettletops or young green peas. In the latter case, the peas are kept whole and added last. For a supper dish, scrambled eggs are often served in the centre; sprinkled with chopped parsley, it will kindle the coldest heart.

After a performance, I'm usually ravenous. I grab for something to fill my stomach, either pasta or starch. I gave up eating red meat a few years back, then decided to cut down on my dairy intake. It took quite a bit of reorganizing of both my daily menu and kitchen set-up. My fridge started housing all sorts of bizzare concoctions to satisfy my post-theatre cravings. (Although I must admit I devour a lot of Cold Sesame Noodles from the local Chinese restaurant!) This lasagna is tasty and satisfying. You'll never miss the beef.

-Robert Hoshour

SPINACH TOFU LASAGNA
serves 2

9 strips lasagna noodles, enough for 3 layers
2 Tbs olive oil
1 large onion, chopped
1/2 lb mushrooms, coarsely chopped
2 cloves garlic, minced
1 package frozen spinach, thawed
2 eggs
8oz Ricotta cheese
8oz tofu
16oz Mozzarella cheese, shredded
1 32oz jar NEWMAN'S OWN spaghetti sauce (Face it, he makes
         good sauce, no sugar or MSG) or YOUR OWN
1 small can tomato sauce, optional if you like a lot of sauce
1/4 cup Parmesan cheese

Preheat oven to 350°.

Cook noodles while you prepare sauce. Adding a tablespoon of olive oil to the water will keep the noodles from sticking together. Do not overcook.

Put 1 Tbs olive oil in a large sauce pan and sauté garlic, onion and mushrooms until tender. Reduce heat, add spinach and simmer a minute. Pour off excess liquid and add mixture to the spaghetti sauce.

Beat eggs slightly in a large bowl, mix in Ricotta cheese and tofu. Stir in the spinach/onion/mushroom combo.

Oil a deep 9" X 9" baking dish and coat the bottom with a bit of sauce to prevent sticking. Layer the noodles, spinach mixture, Mozzarella cheese and sauce, in that order. Repeat layers finishing with noodles. Cover with sauce, sprinkle with Parmesan.

Bake for 45 minutes, let stand 10 minutes before serving.

These pancakes are a "must" with Sauerbraten and delicious with roasts, broiled chicken, and breaded fish. The potatoes should be handled with speed so they won't discolor.

-Uta Hagen

POTATO PANCAKES
serves 6

In a bowl make a batter of:

2 beaten eggs
2 Tbs milk
4 Tbs flour
1 Tbs grated onion
1 Tbs chopped parsley
1 tsp salt

Whisk 'til smooth, cover and set aside.

Then peel 6 large, mature potatoes. Cover them with cold water until ready to grate.

At dinner time grate 2 potatoes at a time on a coarse side of a grater or else the speedy grater of a food processor. Put the grated potatoes in the center of a kitchen towel to twist and squeeze until no more liquid runs out. Stir into the batter at once and proceed with the next two potatoes.

When the batter is finished, melt 1 Tbs butter and 1 Tbs oil. Use a large heavy skillet and a medium-high heat. Add a few spoonfuls of batter to the hot fat using about 1/4 cup per pancake. Cook until golden on each side using a flipper to turn them. Drain on toweling and keep them hot in a warm oven until completed. Add butter to the skillet between batches as needed. Serve at once.

This recipe was reprinted, with permission of the author, from Love For Cooking, © 1976 by Uta Hagen, Collier Books - a division of Macmillan Publishing Co., Inc, New York.

This potato salad recipe is simply sensational. People flip! You might say it's stolen. One time when I was leaving New York I asked the guy at a little Kosher delicatessen for his recipe. I told him I was so hooked on it, I didn't think I could live without it. Naturally, he wouldn't give it to me. It took me eight months to figure out the proper ingredients.
-Phyllis Diller

DILLER'S DELI POTATO SALAD
serves 6-8

Mix
1/4 cup lemon juice
1 tsp sugar
1 cup mayonnaise

Pour over
4 large boiled potatoes, sliced thin

Stir in
2 white cooking onions, diced fine
salt (NO pepper)

Ray Gill
THE WORLD'S BEST POTATO SALAD

5 lbs potatoes
2 medium onions, finely chopped
1/2 tsp salt
1/2 tsp pepper
1/2 tsp white vinegar
16oz jar of mayo (Hellman's is my favorite)

Peel the potatoes. Cut each potato in half, then quarters, and then chunks about 1/2 inch thick. Dump the potato chunks into a pot of boiling water and cook for 10-15 minutes. (Don't overcook or you'll end up with mashed potatoes.) Drain and set aside while you make the "mixture."

The Mixture
Empty the mayo into a large bowl. Add the salt, pepper, vinegar and chopped onions (a cheese grater works best).

While the potatoes are still warm add them to the bowl. Mix carefully, cover with plastic wrap and chill.

★ ☆ ★

These recipes come from Canyon Ranch in Tucson, Arizona. I am always interested in creative low calorie cooking. In my opinion, these potato delights are a very good calorie buy.

-Margo Feiden

VERY SATISFYING BAKED POTATO SKINS
serves 4

4 potatoes

Preheat oven to 425°.

Scrub potatoes well. Slice 1/2 inch thick sections of skin from sides of potato. You should have about 4 slices from each potato. Reserve potato core for another use.

Spread potato skins on ungreased baking sheet. Do not overlap. Bake in pre-heated oven for 1 hour, turning every 20 minutes for even cooking.

The calorie count is approximately 25.8 per ounce.

Margo Feiden
STUFT SPUDS
serves 4

4 small baking potatoes, each approximately 7 ounces
2 medium onions, finely chopped
1/2 cup buttermilk
1 cup low-fat cottage cheese
6 Tbs grated Parmesan or Romano cheese
4 Tbs chopped green onions, including the tops

Wash the potatoes well. Pierce with a fork and bake at 400° for 1 hour.

Cut a very thin slice from the top of each potato. Remove the pulp from the potatoes, being careful not to tear the shells. Mash the potato pulp and set aside in a covered bowl. Keep the shells warm.

Cook the onion, covered, over low heat until soft, stirring occasionally to prevent scorching. Add the mashed potatoes, cottage cheese and all other ingredients except the chopped green onions. Mix well and heat thoroughly. Stuff the potato mixture back into the warm shell. The mixture will be heaping way over the top.

To serve, sprinkle the top of each stuffed potato with 1 tablespoon of chopped green onion. If you have prepared them in advance, heat in a 350° oven for 10 to 15 minutes, or until hot, before adding the chopped onions.

250 calories per serving.

Both the Very Satisfying Baked Potato Skins and Stuft Spuds are used with permission from The Canyon Ranch Cookbook by Jeanne Jones and the Canyon Ranch Staff © 1988 by Sabino Health Resort, Inc. dba The Canyon Ranch.

Uta Hagen
STIR FRIED SPINACH

1 lb fresh spinach, wash the leaves and pat dry on toweling
1 Tbs peanut or light sesame oil
1 or 2 halved cloves of garlic

Coat the bottom of a large heavy pot with the oil; add the garlic. Cook the garlic until it browns pressing down to extract the flavor, then discard. Toss in the spinach leaves. They will snap and crackle with a hell of a noise because of remaining water, but don't worry. Stir the leaves briskly until coated with oil. In less than a minute they will soften and wilt. Then sprinkle with salt, pepper and lemon juice and serve at once.

This recipe was reprinted, with permission of the author, from Love For Cooking, © 1976 by Uta Hagen, Collier Books - a division of Macmillan Publishing Co., Inc., New York.

Maureen McGovern
SPAGHETTI SQUASH PASTA
serves 4

1 spaghetti squash
2 large jars of healthy spaghetti sauce
2 zucchini, diced
1 large onion, chopped
1 small stalk broccoli, in pieces
1 pound mushrooms, sliced
1 carrot, grated
1/4 lb tofu, cubed
3 cloves garlic, minced
fresh basil
dash cayenne

Cook the squash in 2 inches of boiling water, in a skillet, for 20-30 minutes.

For The Sauce
Sauté the zucchini, onion and broccoli lightly. Add mushrooms and garlic and continue to sauté for 2 minutes. Pour the sauce into a medium-sized pot, add the sautéed vegetables, the carrot, tofu, basil and cayenne. Simmer for 30 minutes.

Fork out squash onto warmed plates; cover with sauce.

I have been cooking Indian food for about ten years now, and this is the best spinach dish I have ever tasted. It is terrific with lamb or beef or chicken; and for dinner we often have it with just rice, salad and some Indian bread. It is even better the second day. For that reason, I definitely make it a day ahead for dinner parties.

-Barbara Barrie

PURÉED VEGETABLES
serves 6-8

6oz (or 11/2 cups) chana dal or yellow split peas
3 Tbs vegetable oil
11/4 lb fresh leaf spinach
OR 2 10oz packages frozen leaf spinach
1 medium onion, peeled and coarsley chopped
4 medium tomatoes, chopped
5 fresh, hot chilies
1 tsp salt
3 cups water

Wash the chana dal or split peas well and leave to soak for one hour in about 1 inch of water. Drain. Wash and dry spinach.

Heat the oil in a large pan over a medium-high flame. When hot, put in all ingredients and bring to a boil. Cover, lower heat and boil for one hour. Remove cover, turn heat to high and boil rapidly for another 20 minutes, or until liquid reduces and what remains is a thick stew.

Pour this, in two batches if necessary, into the container of a blender or food processor. Blend. You should end up with a thick purée.

Note: If using chana dal, you must carefully pick through the beans and discard any stone-like bits and foreign bits before washing. Just put small amounts of the chana dal on a platter and push the stones to one side as you examine each group. It doesn't take long, and you can listen to music while you're doing it - Mozart is best.

Francesco Scavullo
STEAMED HERBED VEGETABLES

I prefer vegetables in combination and select them according to season. Zucchini, carrots, green beans, pencil asparagus and broccoli are my favorites. Cut the vegetables attractively and in pieces of similar size to allow them to cook evenly. Steam briefly and garnish with minced mixed fresh herbs or, in Winter, with parsley and freeze-dried chives.

This Zucchini Parmesan is a simple main course that is low calorie but tastes fattening.
-Howard Perloff

ZUCCHINI PARMESAN
serves 4

1 large onion, minced
2 cloves garlic, minced
2 Tbs olive oil
8 to 10 medium zucchini
1 6oz container Ricotta cheese
1/2 cup tomato sauce
1 egg
8oz shredded Mozzarella
salt and pepper, to taste

Wash the zucchini and cut into thin rounds.

Heat oil in a large skillet and sauté the onion and garlic until the onion becomes translucent.

Add the zucchini to the pan and sauté, on a medium-high heat, until tender. Drain the liquid from the pan and lightly brown the zucchini. Remove from the heat and set aside.

Mix together the Ricotta and egg, set aside.

Cover the bottom of a lasagna pan with 1/4 cup tomato sauce. Place a layer of the zucchini/onion mixture in the pan, spoon over a layer of Ricotta cheese, sprinkle with 4oz shredded Mozzarella, salt and pepper. Repeat the process.

Place in a 400° preheated oven and bake for one half hour.

My daughter, Hasna Muhammad, is the most adept cook in our family. Recently she taught me how to make her Stuffed Zucchini. I give it to you, with her permission.

-Ruby Dee

STUFFED ZUCCHINI
serves 4

2 zucchini, acorn squash, eggplant or green peppers
2 cups rice
11/2 tsp tumeric
3 Tbs fresh parsley, chopped
salt, if desired
3 carrots, sliced thin and steamed
1 Tbs butter or oil
1 onion, chopped
1/2 medium green pepper, chopped
1/2 cup mushrooms, sliced
1 lb cooked meat (chicken, beef or even boneless fish)
16oz can tomato puree
handful of fresh spinach
OR 1/2 package frozen spinach
oregano
pepper
garlic powder

Wash and slice zucchini lengthwise. Scoop out enough of the insides to form a cavity. Save what is removed for the sauce. Place the zucchini upside down in a baking dish and cover partially with water. Cover the pan and steam in a 350° oven until tender but not soft. Remove from the oven and set aside.

Cook the rice according to package directions but flavor the water with the tumeric, parsley and salt.

Steam the carrot slices. In a large skillet sauté the onion, green pepper and mushrooms, in 1 Tbs butter or oil, until tender. Add the cooked meat, tomato puree, spinach leaves, and the insides of the squash. Season with oregano, garlic powder, salt and pepper to your liking. Simmer for 5-8 minutes.

Arrange the cooked rice in a baking dish, place the zucchini right side up on top. Fill with the sauce, decorate the rice with the carrot slices, reheat in a moderate oven before serving.

★ ☆ ★

Desserts & Breads

Mom's Bread Pudding
Chocolate Mint Brownies
Maple-Raspberry Custard
Apple Crisp
Carrot Cake
Coffee Cake with Quick Mix Method
Grandma's Skillet Cake
Trifle
(Daddy-Wants-Baby-To-Have-A-Healthy-Colon) Cookie
Pepparkakor
Ice Cream Dream Cake
Sunday Times Crossword Puzzle Ice Cream
Holiday Jello Mold
Fresh Fruit Cobbler
Fudge Pie
Mama's Southern Pecan Pie
Portland Peach Pie
Morning Tofu Pie
Sacher Torte
Cold Soufflé a la Grand Marnier
Banana Nut Bread
Cheese-Mustard Loaf
Cornbread
Irish Soda Bread
Gwen Verdon's Basic Oat Muffins

Mom's bread pudding was my Dad's and my favorite. It lasted all of five minutes whenever she made it. That wasn't too often, I think because she almost never got a chance to get any. I remember it was delicious cold after it had been sitting around a while. My dresser on La Cage, Erna Diaz, always was after me to give some to her, but I never did. So this is for Erna, and in loving memory of my mother, Kay.

-Walter Charles

MOM'S BREAD PUDDING

2 eggs
1/3 cup sugar
1/2 tsp salt
1 tsp vanilla
4 cups milk, scalded
2 cups bread crumbs
1/4 cup melted butter

Preheat oven to 350°.

Pour scalded milk over the bread crumbs and let them soak. Beat eggs just to mix, add sugar, salt and vanilla. Stir the egg mixture into the milk and bread crumbs and add the melted butter. Pour into a greased baking dish and set baking dish into a pan with 1 inch hot water. Bake for 60-75 minutes. It is done when an inserted silver knife comes out clean.

Variations: Add raisins, dates, nuts, lemon peel or chocolate chips. Use left over cake crumbs instead of bread crumbs or use a little of both, works great either way.

I am often called to judge at interschool dance competitions. These competitions go on for several days and at one particularly long event in Connecticut, the moms felt so sorry for the judges they started bringing us "treats." Here's an adaptation of one of my favorites. I brought this to a Valentine's Day party one year and put my friends into a chocolate coma!

- Debra Bier

CHOCOLATE MINT BROWNIES

For The Brownies
1 cup sugar
1/2 cup butter
4 eggs, beaten
1 cup flour
1/2 tsp salt
1 16oz can Hershey's chocolate syrup
1 tsp vanilla
1/2 cup chopped nuts

For The Mint Icing
11/2 cups confectioner's sugar
1/2 cup butter
3 Tbs Creme de Menthe

For The Chocolate Glaze
1 cup chocolate chips
6 Tbs butter

Preheat oven to 350° and grease a 9" X 13" baking pan.

Mix together brownie ingredients, pour into the prepared pan and bake for 25 minutes. Allow to cool. Cream together mint icing ingredients. Spread over cooled cake. Prepare chocolate glaze by melting the chips and butter together. Allow to cool, stirring occasionally to prevent lumping. Spread over mint icing.

Note: Keep in the refrigerator. Take out at least 30 minutes before cutting. Cut into small pieces. A little bit goes a long way!

Robert Morse
MAPLE-RASPBERRY CUSTARD

3 cups heavy cream
6 egg yolks
6 Tbs maple syrup
2 tsp vanilla
1 pint raspberries

Preheat oven to 300°.

Heat cream over a double boiler and add the maple syrup and vanilla. Beat the egg yolks until light and gently pour the hot cream over them, whisk well.

Divide the mixture between 6-8 individual custard cups and place them into a baking dish containing 3 inches of HOT water.

Bake for 35-40 minutes or until a silver knife inserted comes out clean.

Let cool completely.

Top the custards with fresh raspberries, glaze with an extra dollop of maple syrup.

★ ☆ ★

I spent almost a year in the cast of Vampire Lesbians of Sodom. *Other than doing the show, one of my greatest pleasures came from bringing homemade goodies to work. I tried to bake once a week so I could experiment with new recipes and perfect old ones. I wonder if the cast knew they were being used as guinea pigs. They may have been tipped off as I followed them around the dressing room waiting for "oohs and ahs." This recipe is adapted from one I received from a friend and it rated very high on the "Vampires Ooh-Ah Meter."*

-A.J. Vincent

APPLE CRISP

6 apples peeled, cored and sliced- I use different kinds. This adds to the flavor and texture.

Mix
1/2 cup sugar
2 Tbs cinnamon

Mix
1 cup flour
1/2 cup sugar
2 eggs
1/2 cup margarine or butter, melted
1 tsp pure vanilla extract
21/2 Tbs lemon juice

Place apples in a greased 9" X 9" Pyrex pan. Cover the apples with just less than half of the sugar/cinnamon mixture.

Pour second mixture over apples, making sure to cover the entire surface.

With the remaining sugar/cinnamon mixture make a crumb topping by adding bits of margarine or butter (about 1 Tbs in total) to the mixture. Then with your fingers mush the butter into the sugar and crumbs will form. (Trust me.) Sprinkle over the top of the batter.

Bake in a 375° preheated oven for 45 minutes or until the batter is golden brown. Allow to cool slightly before cutting into squares. Serve directly from pan either straight or with a scoop of vanilla ice cream. *Ooh-Ah!*

Both my Carrot Cake and Banana Bread (pg. 203) recipes were given to me by friends but I've added a few touches of my own. I don't really have the patience to see a complicated recipe through so these fall under the category of "Fast and Easy."

- Catherine Ulissey

CARROT CAKE

2 cups sifted flour
2 cups sugar
2 tsp baking soda
1 tsp baking powder
11/2 cups vegetable oil
2 tsp cinnamon
pinch of salt
3 cups grated carrots
4 eggs
1 small can crushed pineapple

Preheat oven to 350°.

In a large bowl, combine the dry ingredients.

In a second large bowl, mix together the remaining ingredients. Slowly add the dry ingredients to the egg mixture.

Pour into a well greased and floured ring pan. Bake for approximately 11/2 hours. Check after 1 hour; when an inserted toothpick comes out clean, it is done.

Allow to cool before applying the frosting.

Cream Cheese Frosting
1 box confectioner's sugar
1/2 cup sweet butter
8oz cream cheese
pinch of salt
1/2 tsp vanilla

Mix the cream cheese with the butter, add the sugar and beat well. Mix in the salt and vanilla.

After frosting the cake, dust the top with some crushed nuts.

★ ☆ ★

When I was attending Alexander Hamilton High School in Los Angeles, one of my favorite things was the coffee cake they served in the school cafeteria. I couldn't resist it. I mean, it was heaven! Suzie loved it as much as I did. She was my best friend; still is. We even asked for the recipe, but they wouldn't give it to us. Not long ago, Suzie and I were reminiscing about our days at "Hammie High" and decided to go have lunch in the cafeteria, for old times sake (we graduated in 1960). We really wanted to see if they still served that coffee cake. They did, and it was still heaven. This time when I asked for the recipe they let me have it. I guess a few Broadway shows, movies and a television series gave me a little more stature than I'd had before. Anyway, here it is; just as they gave it to me; just as I make it because I haven't the foggiest idea of how to break it down. It helps having lots of friends to share with... and a series (Knots Landing) with a large cast and crew.

-Michele Lee

COFFEE CAKE WITH QUICK MIX METHOD

1 lb yeast, compressed
31/2 quarts lukewarm water (variable)
10 to 11 lbs Bakers' flour
2 lbs cake flour
15oz dry milk powder
2 lbs granulated sugar
4oz salt
1/2 to 1oz nutmeg (optional)
2 lbs shortening
1 lb eggs, slightly beaten

Yeild: Approximately 27 lbs of dough

1. Dissolve yeast in part of the lukewarm water. A bowl with a rounded bottom is the best to use for dissolving the yeast.
2. Blend dry ingredients and shortening in mixer bowl.
3. Add yeast/water mixture to the mixer bowl, then the eggs and remaining water. Mix only long enough for the flour to be well incorporated. A dough hook is recommended for the entire mixing process.
4. Scale off dough in 4 lb pieces. Place on greased bun pans.
5. Roll out in rectangular shape.
6. Brush with 1/4 cup (2oz) melted butter or margarine. Sprinkle with one cup (6oz) crumb filling (see next page).
7. Roll up like a jelly roll. Cut into standard size pieces.
8. Place on greased bun pans. Pat out.
9. Let rise until dough doubles in size. Bake at 400° for 8-10 minutes.
10. When partially cool, brush with glaze (see next page).

Crumb Filling
10 lbs bread crumbs
10 lbs brown sugar
1 cup cinnamon

Combine ingredients. Mix thoroughly.

Sugar Glaze
6 lbs powdered sugar
2 cups hot water
1 Tbs vanilla

Combine all ingredients, beat throughly.
Yeild: 2 quarts plus 1/2 cup

Note: The glaze will thicken as it stands. Thin to proper consistency with water.
Egg shade food coloring added to the glaze will improve the color.

*My mother passed this recipe on to me. It is so easy you won't believe how good it tastes.
I make it in the morning and take it to rehearsal for the cast to munch with their coffee.
It reminds everyone of their grandma's baking.*

- Marcia Mitzman

GRANDMA'S SKILLET CAKE

1 cup sugar
1 cup flour
3 eggs
1/4 lb butter (1 stick)
1 tsp vanilla

Melt butter in a round cake pan and let cool to room temperature.

Sift flour and sugar into a large bowl. Mix in the butter, eggs and vanilla until it makes a smooth batter.

Pour into the cake pan which is already buttered. Bake in a preheated oven at 350° for 20-25 minutes or until the edges are golden brown.

Very good and so easy!

Michael Crawford
TRIFLE
serves 10

2 8-inch round, stale pound cakes
2 pkg frozen strawberries
1 pkg Bird's English custard, follow package directions
OR 1 pkg Jello vanilla pudding, slightly sweetened
1/2 pint cream, whipped and slightly sweetened
12 whole, fresh, perfect strawberries
1/2 cup sherry (or rum)

Split cake layers in half horizontally. Place the first layer in the bottom of a deep (4 Quart) trifle bowl*. Sprinkle liberally with sherry. Spread 1/2 pkg of frozen strawberries on the cake then drizzle with 1/4 pkg of the English custard. Repeat the above steps with each of the three remaining layers. Spread top with whipped cream. Garnish with fresh berries and chill.

A trifle bowl is a large glass serving bowl. -Ed.

Andre DeShields
(Daddy-Wants-Baby-To-Have-A-Healthy-Colon) COOKIE

Dry Ingredients
1 cup mixed nuts and seeds, ground in a blender
2 cups instant oatmeal (Old Wessex Ltd.)
1/2 cup 5-grain cereal (American Prairie)
1/2 cup whole wheat pastry flour
2 Tbs soy flour
1/2 tsp sea salt
1 tsp baking soda
1 tsp baking powder

Wet Ingredients
1/2 cup peanut oil (cold-pressed and unrefined)
1 Tbs lecithin
1 cup maple syrup
1 tsp vanilla
2 tsp egg replacer (Ener-G) dissolved in 4 Tbs water

Final Ingredients
1 cup soy milk (I use vanilla Edensoy)
1 cup raisins (manukka are dark, plump and naturally sweet)

Preheat oven to 350°.

With a wire whisk, and in a large bowl, blend together all the dry ingredients. In a second large bowl, but with the same whisk, cream the wet ingredients until smooth and fully blended. In small portions, add the dry to the wet. You'll end up with a stiff porridge. Now, stir in the soy milk followed by the raisins.

Drop the batter by spoonfulls onto an ungreased cookie sheet. Bake on the middle shelf of the oven for 15-20 minutes or until golden in color. Let cool on the cookie sheet a few minutes before removing.

This recipe will make 1 dozen 5 inch cookies (my preference) or 3 dozen 2 inch ones.

Health and happiness!

My mother's side of the family is Swedish and this recipe has been passed down from my Great Grandmother. In Swedish, Pepparkakor means "Brown Pepper Cookie" and pepper means spicy. These have been a holiday favorite in our family for years.

-Deborah Graham

PEPPARKAKOR

2 cups light molasses
1/2 lb butter
2 cups sugar
1 tsp ginger
1 tsp clove
1 Tbs orange peel, finely chopped
3 eggs, well beaten
1 tsp baking soda
7 cups flour (or as needed to make a stiff dough)
colored sugar (optional)

Cook molasses to the boiling point then take off of burner and melt the butter in the molasses. Pour the buttered molasses into a large mixing bowl and add the sugar, ginger, clove, orange peel, eggs and soda. Beat well with the addition of each ingredient. Add flour gradually until a stiff dough forms. Let the dough stand in the refrigerator overnight.

Onto a lightly floured board, roll small portions of dough very thin. Cut into desired shapes. Place on a buttered cookie sheet (no need to butter between batches). Sprinkle with colored sugars if desired and bake 8-10 minutes in a 350° oven. Yields about 300 cookies.

This is a variation of an old recipe of my mother's. I had actually forgotten about it until I was about to be engaged and was planning a dinner for my family to meet my soon to be fiancé's family. When it came to planning the dessert, I was stumped. It had to be easy because the meal I was planning was extremely detailed. It also had to be special and beautiful considering the occasion.

I then remembered something similar my mother had made. I added the macaroons, put it in a fancy mold and the next night it was perfect! I've had nothing but raves on it ever since. My wife and I regard it as our "engagement treat."

-Rex Smith

ICE CREAM DREAM CAKE

1 gallon gourmet vanilla ice cream (or get creative and experiment!)
8oz fresh whipped cream or Cool Whip
6-8 macaroons
your favorite fruit

Let the ice cream melt to a mixable consistancy. Add the whipped cream and blend thoroughly. Crumble the macaroons and add to the ice cream/whipped cream mixture.

Grease a favorite mold or cake pan (PAM works best) and pour in batter. Let it set in your freezer overnight.

Just before serving, purée your favorite fruit (berries are great and add nice color) and spoon over slices of the "cake."

It's delicious, easy and beautiful!

Bebe Neuwirth
SUNDAY TIMES CROSSWORD PUZZLE ICE CREAM
serves 2

1 pint Haagen-Daz Chocolate-Chocolate Chip ice cream
1 package Reese's Peanut Butter Cups

Place one peanut butter cup in one bowl, and the other in your partner's bowl. Mash the first one. Mash the second. This is easier if you break each cup into little pieces first.

Put 1/2 pint of ice cream in one bowl. Mush it together with the peanut butter cup smithereens. Put the other 1/2 pint of ice cream in second bowl. Repeat the mushing step from the first bowl.

Eat while doing the Sunday Times Crossword Puzzle late at night.

Lynne Taylor-Corbet
HOLIDAY JELLO MOLD

1 large package raspberry Jello
1 envelope pure, unflavored gelatin
1 cup hot water
1 can whole, jellied cranberries
1 box frozen raspberries
1/2 cup celery, chopped
rind of 1/2 an orange, boiled and chopped
OR 1 small can mandarin oranges, drained
1/2 cup chopped almonds or walnuts
1/2 cup cold water

Dissolve Jello and gelatin in hot water. Stir well. Add the cranberries and raspberries along with their juices. Mix in the celery, orange rind or slices and chopped nuts. Keep stirring as you add the cold water.

Prepare the Jello mold by coating lightly with mayonnaise. Pour the batter into the mold, refrigerate 2-3 hours or until very firm. Release from mold onto a lettuce dressed platter.

It's a big hit every time!

Maureen McGovern
FRESH FRUIT COBBLER

1 pint blueberries
6-8 fresh peaches
1/2 cup raisins
1/4 cup apple, apricot or peach juice
1 tsp cinnamon
1 cup rolled oats
1/2 cup chopped almonds
2 Tbs sesame seeds
1/4 cup sunflower seeds
4 Tbs safflower oil
nutmeg

Mix friuts and juice and put into a greased 13" X 9" baking dish. Sprinkle with cinnamon.

Mix oats, nuts and seeds with a fork or pastry cutter, add the oil. Put over fruit and sprinkle with nutmeg.

Bake at 350° for 1 hour.

This recipe makes me very popular at parties. It's great because it really is delicious and you only have to dirty one pan.

-Liz Callaway

FUDGE PIE

1/4 cup (1/2 stick) butter
12oz semi-sweet chocolate chips
1/4 cup rum
3/4 cup firmly packed brown sugar
2 tsp instant coffee granules or espresso powder
3 eggs
1/4 cup all-purpose flour
1 cup chopped walnuts
1 9-inch pie crust (store bought chocolate wafer is the best but frozen is OK)

Preheat oven to 350°.

In a small sauce pan, melt the butter and chocolate chips over a low heat. Stir occasionally. Stir in the rum, brown sugar, coffee granules, eggs and flour. You must mix the ingredients IN THAT ORDER to insure proper results. The mixture should be stirred until smooth, then add the chopped walnuts. Next, pour into the pie shell and bake for 25 minutes or until the filling is puffed up and the crust is light brown. Cool completely before serving. Fresh whipped cream or vanilla ice cream makes a great topper.

My mother, Bertye T. Bates, always fixed this delicious pie (a southern favorite) for my visits home. One Fall I made two of these for a dinner at Beth Henley's house.

-Kathy Bates

MAMA'S SOUTHERN PECAN PIE

3 whole eggs
2 Tbs melted butter or margarine
2 Tbs flour
1/4 tsp vanilla
1/8 tsp salt
1/2 cup sugar
11/2 cup dark corn syrup
11/2 cup broken pecan halves
1 unbaked 8-inch pie shell

Beat eggs. Blend in melted butter, flour, vanilla, salt, sugar and syrup. Sprinkle nuts over the bottom of the pie shell and gently pour in the liquid. Bake in a preheated 425° oven for 10 minutes, then reduce heat to 325° and bake for an additional 40 minutes.

Not too many people think of peaches when they think of Portland... it's usually apples that get the press! But we had two huge peach trees in our back yard and, every year, I couldn't wait for the peaches to ripen so I could help mother (Mother Struthers) make her famous peach pies. I would always take a bag of peaches to all the neighbors on the block.

-Sally Struthers

PORTLAND PEACH PIE

2 cups milk
2 eggs
1/2 cup sugar
3 Tbs cornstarch
dash of salt
1/2 tsp vanilla
pat of butter
4-6 peaches, cut into thick slices
a graham cracker crust
fresh whipped cream*

In a medium saucepan, mix milk and eggs with a beater. In a separate bowl combine the sugar, cornstarch and salt and slowly pour the dry ingredients into the egg mixture, stir with a wooden spoon. Cook over a medium heat, stirring constantly until the mixture boils and thickens. Remove from the heat, add the vanilla and the butter and let cool. Arrange the peach slices in the crust. Pour the cooled mixture over them. Cover with whipped cream and store in refrigerator until set.

*To make whipped cream place a medium-sized metal bowl and the beaters from your mixer in the freezer for about ten minutes. Take them out and pour 1/2 pint heavy cream (or more, depending on the size of the pie shell) into the bowl along with 2 Tbs sugar and 1/2 tsp vanilla. Beat until stiff but not dry.

Graham Cracker Crust
11/2 cups graham cracker crumbs
4 Tbs butter, melted
2 Tbs sugar
scant 1/4 tsp nutmeg

Blend all ingredients well and turn into a 9-inch glass pie plate. Press onto the bottom and up the sides of the pan. Make sure the edge is not too thin and that there are no loose crumbs.

Place pan on a cookie sheet and bake in the center of a 375° oven for 8 minutes, or until the edges are golden brown.

Cool, and then refrigerate for 30 minutes before filling.

OK. *You wake up in the morning - HUNGRY! And your sweet tooth is gnawing at your tastebuds. But you daren't grab for the Frosted Flakes... this is the new-age of enlightened, health-conscious, fit-for-everything (even swinging from a trapeze) performing super-stars. What can be gobbled??? MORNING TOFU PIE! Tofu is fairly bland without some sort of doctoring. Yet it supplies lots of protein and no dairy. What follows is a favorite, flavorful dish that is sweet (yet not decadent) and very simple to make.*

-Robert Hoshour

MORNING TOFU PIE

2 medium tart apples (Granny Smith)
2 tofu cakes (1/2 lb)
1/4 cup plain low-fat yogurt
1 to 2 Tbs honey, maple syrup or molasses
1 to 2 Tbs lemon juice, to taste
1/2 tsp ground cinnamon
1/2 tsp nutmeg
1 Tbs sesame tahini
1 tsp vanilla
2 tsp whole wheat pastry flour

Preheat oven to 350°.
Either prepare a crust or butter a 1 quart baking dish. (A simple crust can be quickly prepared by mixing two cups of granola with 1/2 stick of melted butter in a deep dish pie pan and pressing into shape. Refrigerate until ready to use.)

Quarter and core apples, steam until soft. (You'll need to add a veggie steamer to your kitchen supplies.) Place all ingredients in a blender. Blend until smooth. Pour mixture into crust or baking dish.

Bake for 30-40 minutes, until firm and just beginning to brown. Cool and refrigerate. If you've used a crust, cover the top with a thick layer of apple butter or your favorite jam.

John Simon and Patricia Hoag
SACHER TORTE

1/3 cup butter at room temperature
6 Tbs sugar
3oz semi-sweet chocolate pieces, melted
4 egg yolks
1/2 cup plus 1 Tbs sifted flour
5 egg whites
21/2 Tbs apricot jam
chocolate icing (see below)

Grease and flour an 8-inch spring form cake pan.

Preheat oven to 325°.

Cream together the butter and the sugar until pale yellow in color and fluffy. Add the melted chocolate pieces and mix. Add the egg yolks one at a time, mixing well after each addition. Blend in the flour.

In a separate bowl, beat the egg whites until they are stiff and form peaks. Fold them into the batter. Pour the mixture into the prepared pan and bake for one hour and fifteen minutes. Remove and let stand for 15 minutes before attempting to unspring the pan.

After the cake has cooled completely, spread the top with the jam. Pour chocolate icing over the cake so that it coats the top and sides.

Chocolate Icing
6 1oz squares semi-sweet baking chocolate
1/2 cup light cream
2 sticks butter (1 cup)
21/2 cup confectioner's sugar

In a sauce pan, combine the chocolate, cream and butter. Melt over a low flame and stir until smooth. Remove from heat. Add the confectioner's sugar, a little at a time, and whisk until blended.

Set the pan in a larger bowl that has been filled with ice and beat (on high speed) until the frosting is of a thick but pourable consistancy.

This dessert is thinning, of course! It is a favorite of mine and my husband, Richard Merrell. At first you may think all that liquor is a mistake. It's not - it's divine.

-Jan Miner

COLD SOUFFLÉ a la GRAND MARNIER

10 macaroons (see below or store bought)
3/4 cup plus 6 Tbs Grand Marnier
2 Tbs orange juice concentrate
grated rind of 1 orange
5 eggs
2/3 cup sugar
2 cups heavy cream

In a bowl mix macaroons, 3 Tbs Grand Marnier, 2 Tbs orange juice concentrate and mash into a paste. Separate 4 eggs and save the whites. In a large bowl, beat the egg yolks and the remaining whole egg with 2/3 cup sugar until light and thick. Stir in 3 Tbs Grand Marnier and the grated rind. Whip the heavy cream and fold into the egg yolk mixture. Whip the 4 egg whites until stiff and fold into the egg yolk & cream mixture.

Spread 1/2 of the macaroon paste on the bottom of a 9-inch spring form pan. Pour in 1/2 of the egg & cream mixture. Make another layer with the remaining macaroon paste and pour in the remaining egg & cream mixture. Freeze at least 4 hours.

Remove from freezer 30 minutes before serving and release from spring form pan. When ready to serve, heat the 3/4 cup Grand Marnier, pour over the soufflé and flambé.

One last step. Share the rest of the bottle of Grand Marnier with your guests and take two aspirins in the morning.

Coconut Macaroons
1/3 cup all-purpose flour
21/2 cups shredded coconut (packaged is better than fresh in this case)
1/8 tsp salt
2/3 cup sweetened condensed milk
1 tsp vanilla

Preheat oven to 350°.

Mix flour, shredded coconut and salt in a large bowl. Pour in the condensed milk and the vanilla and stir into a thick batter. (Stir by hand, an electric mixer will over mix the batter.) Drop the batter by 1/4 cupfuls onto a greased cookie sheet. Leave approximately one inch of space between drops because they will swell during baking. Bake for 20 minutes or until golden brown. Yields 18 cookies. Be sure to let the cookies cool completely (or even let them sit out for several hours) before mashing.

Catherine Ulissey
BANANA NUT BREAD

2 cups sifted cake flour
11/2 cups sugar
1/2 cup shortening
2 eggs
3 ripe bananas, mashed with a fork
11/2 tsp vanilla
1 tsp salt
1 tsp baking soda
4 heaping Tbs sour cream
1 cup nuts (walnuts or pecans)

Preheat oven to 350°.

Cream together the sugar and the shortening. Beat in the eggs, sour cream, bananas and vanilla. Blend the dry ingredients, add to the wet and mix well. Stir in the nuts last.

Pour the batter into a greased and floured loaf pan. Bake 1 hour.

The Patchword Seder

Years ago, when the week's activity consisted of four days of making rounds and one day at the unemployment office, several friends and I would get our families together for communal holiday celebrations.

When Passover came around, we had an invitational seder. The responsibility of preparing the main dish was ours, but it was the other dishes that provided the excitement. Mrs. Joe Raposo was to bring the chicken soup (I mean, zuppa alla cacciatore); chicken soup is a bit extreme for the ordinary seder table! Her arangi matzo balls... incredible! And Mrs. Dick O'Neill's charoses*- every year those same delicious charoses. It was so good that no one ever asked her how come it was green.

This recipe was our contribution at Christmas tree-trimming time. I especially recommend it for unemployed actors.

-Hal Linden

*Charoses is a paste-like mixture of apples, nuts, cinnamon and wine used during the Seder meals at Passover. It is symbolic of the clay the Israelites used to make bricks during their Egyptian slavery. -Ed.

CHEESE-MUSTARD LOAF

1 loaf unsliced bakery bread (day old cuts best)
1/2 pound (8 slices) Jack cheese
1/2 pound (8 slices) American cheese
1 cup softened butter or margarine
2/3 cup finely minced onions
6 Tbs prepared mustard
2 Tbs poppy seeds
4 tsp lemon juice
1/2 tsp monosodium glutamate (optional)

Make eight diagonal, equal cuts in bread almost to the bottom. Mix butter, onions, mustard, poppy seeds and lemon juice. Spread a few tablespoons of mixture into slices. Reserve the rest. Sprinkle cheese slices with monosodium glutamate. Place one slice of each cheese in each cut. Press bread together (tie with string for firm hold). Place in shallow greased baking pan or on cookie sheet. Spread rest of butter mixture on top and sides of bread. Bake in 350° oven for 20 minutes, or until slightly brown and cheese has melted. Serve with salad. Makes 9 slices.

★ ☆ ★

CORNBREAD
for Mom's Chili

3/4 cup cornmeal
1 cup whole wheat flour
1/3 cup sugar
3 tsp baking powder
1/2 tsp salt
1 cup buttermilk
1 egg, well beaten
2 Tbs butter or margarine, melted

Combine all the dry ingredients in a large bowl. Add the buttermilk, egg and butter; beat well.

Spoon into a greased 8-inch square cake pan or muffin tins and bake in a 425°, preheated oven for 20 minutes. Cool completely and cut into 2-inch squares.

David Birney
IRISH SODA BREAD
from Mother Jeanne's Kitchen

3 cups whole wheat flour
11/2 cups white flour
41/2oz bran (or wheat germ)
1 rounded tsp baking soda
1 level tsp baking powder
1 tsp salt
1 rounded tsp sugar
almost 2 cups buttermilk

Mix all ingredients in a large bowl.

Knead on a floured board. Round dough. Divide in two. Form two loaves, one inch thick and seven inches in diameter.

Sharp cut an X on top. Place on a floured tray and bake at 400° for 35 minutes.

Serve warm with butter.

Gwen Verdon's
BASIC OAT MUFFINS
yields 1 dozen

11/4 cups Quaker Whole Oats (not instant), put in a blender
    to make coarse flour
11/4 cups Quaker Whole Bran
2 small packages of Sweet 'N Low
1/2 cup raisins
2 tsp baking powder
11/4 cups skim milk
4 egg whites, beaten until stiff
1 Tbs safflower oil or vegetable oil
1 heaping tsp cinnamon
1 tsp vanilla

Preheat oven to 425°.

Mix dry ingredients in a bowl. Add all the wet ingredients except the egg whites. Mix thoroughly and fold in the beaten egg whites. Place paper cups in muffin pan wells, spoon batter in. Bake for 17 minutes. When you remove them from the oven, leave muffins in pan for 2 minutes. Remove and place upside down on a cooling rack.

Enjoy!

Miscellaneous

Betty Beer
Jackie Mason's Perfect Egg Cream
Curry and Cheddar Scrambled Eggs
Eggs Birmingham
Cheese Enchiladas
New England Red Flannel Hash
Made to Order
Matzo Brei
Lennie Gershe's Mystery Lunch Delight
The McGovern Peanut Butter Sandwich
Thomsen's Famous Michigan Relish
Joan Rivers' Toast

One of the great adventures of my married life with Larry Parks was our beer-making experience. Larry had tasted some home-made beer made by a friend of his from the gym where he worked out. He came home all fired-up with the idea of making beer. We bought a 12-gallon crock, a mash & brew tester, bottles, caps, a bottle capper and all the ingredients. We followed the directions explicitly, and then watched for our beer to brew. As you can see from the recipe, it's a touchy matter to pick the exact moment when the beer is ready to bottle. The mash & brew tester is like a thermometer that floats atop the beer. If you bottle before the thermometer sinks to the red line, the beer will keep brewing and you'll have a lot of exploding bottles in your cellar. If you wait too long, your beer will be flat. We had no idea how long it took for the tester to reach the red line, so Larry and I went to bed and set the alarm for every half hour and took turns getting up. After checking the progress, we'd sneak back into bed whispering "not ready yet." At six in the morning it hit the red line and we bottled I can't remember how many bottles of the most delicious beer I've ever tasted. We couldn't wait the three weeks to try one bottle.

Warning: This beer is much stronger than commercial beer and can knock you for a loop, but boy, is it good!

-Betty Garrett

BETTY BEER

8 lbs corn sugar (never use cane or beet sugar)
1 bag seedless hops
2 envelopes Knox Gelatin (optional)
1 can Supreme Malt
1 yeast cake
12 gallon porcelain crock
beer bottles, either pint or quart (Be sure bottles are
      clean. Dirty bottles can spoil your beer.)
bottle caps
bottle capper (Can be purchased from a restaurant supply
      store, I think.)
Mash and Brew Tester
Rubber tubing, to syphon beer from crock to bottles

Dissolve Supreme Malt in 4 cups boiling water. Put the dissolved malt and corn sugar in the crock. Put hops in a cloth and tie with string to make a large tea bag. Put the bag into a medium-sized pot of hot water and simmer for 10 minutes. Do not boil hops. Squeeze bag of excess water, allow to drain, throw bag away and pour hops liquid into the crock. Fill crock within two inches of the top. This will cool the solution to lukewarm.

Dissolve yeast cake in one cup of lukewarm water and add this to the brew. Stir. Let sit.

The first morning, skim off the froth from the top of crock with a spoon. Do not molest until ready to bottle.

For accuracy use Mash and Brew Tester to tell when to bottle. The level should meet the red line. If you wait too long and the tester sinks past the red line, add 1/4 tsp corn sugar to pint bottles or 1/2 tsp to quart bottles. This will keep the brew from being flat.

Gelatin may be used to settle the yeast. Thoroughly dissolve 2 envelopes Knox Gelatin into a sauce pan of 1 pint warm water. Pour over top of brew in crock a day or two before bottling.

After bottling, let stand at least three weeks before using. After two, three, four months the brew will become 100% better and stronger.

Do not use aluminum pots when you simmer hops; it takes on a metallic taste.

Kids today discuss who's the best baseball player. Adults decide who's the best president. But when I was a kid, people would stand around on the corner arguing about which guy in which candy store made the best egg cream. You would think they were debating who started World War II.

It was always one of the big accomplishments, who made the best egg cream. I'm such a genius with an egg cream. It's like when you watched your Jewish or Italian mother making dinner. They never had formulas or written measurements. By instinct, they made the thing perfect every time. Same thing with me. Somehow if I make 200 egg creams, they'll all taste exactly the same. It's amazing how I'm never wrong. I can't get over it myself.

JACKIE'S SECRET: The main thing about an egg cream is that it should have a good quality milk chocolate and a powerhouse fizz. A 'pushy' seltzer is much better than a standard seltzer because it creates a bigger head.

-Jackie Mason

JACKIE MASON'S PERFECT EGG CREAM

"Fox's U-Bet" Chocolate Flavor Syrup
Whole Milk

Seltzer (preferably the old-fashioned, cobalt blue, 'pushy' bottle)
Iced tea spoon

Pour "this much" syrup (about half an inch) into a tall glass. Add "this much" milk (2-3 inches). Hold seltzer bottle six inches from glass and fill with a "powerhouse fizz" of seltzer. Stir with the long spoon and enjoy the winner of The Lower East Side Egg Cream Wars.

Much gratitude must go to my wife who was unwittingly subjected to several curry experiments of my devising. She would eat whatever I placed in front of her, but often her face glowed red and sweat broke out on her forehead. I knew I had hit the right combination of ingredients when her face finally glowed from contentment, not combustion.

-Nick Kaledin

CURRY AND CHEDDAR SCRAMBLED EGGS

eggs - 2 per person
curry powder
freshly ground black pepper
salt
1oz grated Sharp Cheddar cheese per serving
butter

Beat eggs in a bowl. Add salt, pepper and a pinch of curry powder. Careful not to overdo it with the curry powder, it can be overpowering. Mix in the grated cheese.

Melt butter in a pan and scramble mixture over medium-high heat until cooked to your desired taste.

Great for brunch or a light supper with sliced French bread and a Caesar Salad.

Eli Wallach
EGGS BIRMINGHAM

Eggs Birmingham were first mentioned in Tennessee Williams' one-act play *The Unsatisfactory Supper*. Get two slices of bread (whole wheat or white), cut a hole in the center. Place in a frying pan or omelette pan, drop an egg into the hole, cover the pan with a lid until done. Serve with a piece of bread on top of the yellow of the egg.

Debbie Reynolds
CHEESE ENCHILADAS
makes 1 dozen

1 dozen tortillas
1/2 lb Longhorn cheese, medium grated
1/2 lb Jack cheese, medium grated
1 medium onion, chopped
1/4 cup oil
2 Tbs flour
2 small cans tomato sauce
salt, pepper, chili powder

Fry onion in oil until clear. Add flour, then tomato sauce, plus two cans of water (make like gravy). Add salt, pepper and chili powder to taste.

Warm the tortillas, dip into sauce, fill with cheese and roll. Place all 12 in casserole and top with rest of sauce and cheese. Bake 15 minutes in 350° oven.

This is an early junk food and it is pure pleasure; a treat for the stomach and the eyes. It was first served to me by my grandfather in Vermont. His whole world was New England. He used to warn me against southerners. "Stay away from Hartford," he'd say. Grandpa had a large garden. He'd put a cauldron of water on the wood burning stove and when it was boiling he'd pull out his pocket watch and say "Run down to the corn field and bring back 18 ears. Not too big, not too small. If you can get them picked, husked and into the pot within ten minutes, they'll be worth eating." Once a week, my grandmother would bake bread and a wonderful aroma would fill the house. There were no frozen dinners, prepared entrees or ready mixes back then. The preparation of food filled a large part of the day and made the consumption of it an important and marvelously enjoyable event.

-Orson Bean

NEW ENGLAND RED FLANNEL HASH

Open one can of hash (my favorite brand: Broadcast). Open one small can of diced beets. Mix the hash and the beets, include enough of the beet juice to color the hash a fine, bright red. Fry or broil.

Carol Burnett
MADE TO ORDER
serves 1-200

Wolf's Sixth Avenue Delicatessen
101 West 57th Street
NY, NY 10019
(212) 586-1110

THEY DELIVER!

I needed something to eat Wednesday and Saturday mornings to get me through the matinee performances of Sugar. *This simple meal in the morning would last all through the show. If, perhaps, it didn't, I would augment with a candy bar. Well, "nobody's perfect!"*

-Elaine Joyce

MATZO BREI
serves 3

6 sheets matzo
4 eggs
1 Tbs butter
cold water

Soak the matzo in cold water until soft. In a separate bowl, beat the eggs with a little salt. Squeeze the water out of the matzo and pour in the eggs. Let soak. Melt the butter in a skillet and scramble the matzo/egg mixture to the desired consistancy.

Serve with apple sauce or syrup.

This was first served to my husband, Bruce Paltrow, and me by Lennie Gershe. This wonderful man wrote Butterflies are Free, *my first Broadway play. I added it to my repertoire and it's been a mainstay ever since. Lennie Gershe's contributions to my culinary repertoire continue to delight and mystify.*

-Blythe Danner

LENNIE GERSHE'S MYSTERY LUNCH DELIGHT

1 can chopped ripe olives
4 scallions, chopped, including greens
grated Sharp or Cheddar cheese
a few dashes of Worcestershire sauce

1 tsp curry powder
2 Tbs mayo
1 English Muffin, per person, toasted

Mix all ingredients together and spread on a toasted English Muffin. Place under a broiler, open-faced, 'til brown.

The McGovern Peanut Butter, Lettuce, Tomato and Onion Sandwich was a favorite of my father's (James McGovern) as a child, obviously passed down through generations from the old country, as it were.

Yes, indeed, as the good ol' lore would have it, literally thousands were saved from the great peanut butter famine at the turn of the century by one ingenious young man, "Terrible Terry McGovern" (a pugilist by trade). He, having great foresight, stockpiled, yes, stockpiled, gallons of smooth and chunky peanut butter, thus saving the human race from a fate worse than... well, you know the rest.

-Maureen McGovern

THE McGOVERN PEANUT BUTTER SANDWICH

2 slices bread (7 grain or white, if you must)
peanut butter, smooth or crunchy
1 lettuce leaf
tomato, sliced
onion slice (more or less to taste)

Spread peanut butter on bread, add lettuce, tomato and onion and — Enjoy!

Trust me, it doesn't taste as bad as it sounds... it's great!!!!

"If this don't turn your head - nothin' will," is a common saying in reference to this relish in Lansing, Michigan. The original recipe was taught to me by R. Thomsen himself, a chef of the first order and a curmudgeon to boot. I guarantee this to be the busiest serving dish on the Thanksgiving table.

-Jeffrey DeMunn

THOMSEN'S FAMOUS MICHIGAN RELISH

2 lbs cranberries
1 medium onion
1 Tbs horseradish, heaping and fresh
1 or 2 Tbs sugar

Mix like hell in a food processor and chill.

Add 12oz or so of sour cream before serving.

This recipe has been in my family for generations.

-Joan Rivers

JOAN RIVERS' TOAST
Serves 2

2 slices white bread
butter or margarine

Take two slices of white bread, place them in a toaster. Press down the handle. Wait two minutes or until toast pops up.

Spread butter over slices AFTER removing them from the toaster.

For holidays and special occasions, raisin bread may be substituted, but follow the same procedure as above. For these special occasions we call it "Joan Rivers' Holiday Toast."

Measuring Equivalents

a pinch ★ less than 1/8 teaspoon

a dash ★ a few drops

3 teaspoons ★ 1 tablespoon

4 tablespoons ★ 1/4 cup

5 tablespoons plus 1 teaspoon ★ 1/3 cup

16 tablespoons ★ 1 cup

2 cups ★ 1 pint

4 cups ★ 1 quart

2 pints ★ 1 quart

4 quarts ★ 1 gallon

1 fluid ounce ★ 2 tablespoons

8 fluid ounces ★ 1 cup

16 dry ounces ★ 1 pound

one 4 ounce stick butter ★ 8 tablespoons

4 cups sifted flour ★ 1 pound

2 cups granulated sugar ★ 1 pound

Baking Times and Temperatures

	Temp °F	Minutes
Breads		
Biscuits	425-450	10-15
Corn Bread	400-425	30-40
Cream Puffs	375	60
Quick Loaf Breads	350-375	60-75
Yeast Breads	400	30-40
Sweet Rolls	375	20-30
Cakes		
Cup	350-375	15-25
Layer	350-375	20-35
Loaf	350	45-60
Angel food	350-375	30-45
Cookies		
Drop	350-400	8-15
Rolled	375	8-10
Eggs, Milk and Cheese Dishes	350	30-60
Custard	350	30-60
Macaroni and Cheese	350	25-30
Meat Loaf	300	50-90
Meat Pie	400	25-30
Meats	350	30-60
Pastry		
One Crust Pie (Custard)	400	30-40
Shell Only	450	10-12
Two Crust (uncooked filling)	400	45-55
Two Crust (cooked filling)	425-450	30-45

Index

Photo Credits

Ed Asner's photo by Dana Gluckstein
Phyllis Diller's photo by Marc Raboy
Arthur Faria's photo by Roy Blakey
Margo Feiden's drawing by Al Hirschfeld
Harvey Fierstein's photo by Michael Paris
Helen Hayes' photo courtesy of Walt Disney Productions
Al Hirschfeld's self portrait courtesy of the Margo Feiden Galleries
Sylvia Miles' photo by Jack Mitchell
Debbie Reynolds' photo by Harry Langdon
Joan Rivers' photo by Harry Langdon
Francesco Scavullo's photo by Sean M. Byrnes
John Simon's photo by Jody Caravaglia
Lynne Taylor-Corbett's photo by Gordon Meyer
A.J. Vincent's photo by Francesco Scavullo

Notes

Notes

Notes

Notes

Notes

Don't miss our other fine titles!

The Insider's Guide To Modeling: The Pros Tell You How
$14.95 Cloth.
Top professionals in the modeling business, including Agents, Models, Photographers, and Hair and Makeup artists, tell how to break into this lucrative field.

How To Succeed As A Male Model
$12.95 Paper
This comprehensive guide provides all the information necessary to make it as a male model. Included are many interviews with working models who reveal their secrets to success!

Staying Thin: The Model's Health & Fitness Regimen
$14.95 Cloth
Models have to stay thin and healthy, and this book will show you how to do it! This sensible diet and exercise plan is easy to follow and can be used by everyone.

The Staying Thin Cookbook
$16.95 Cloth
Over 150 delicious low-calorie recipes to be used with the Staying Thin Regimen, or with any health & fitness plan.

Staying Thin For Kids: The Family Guide To Health & Fitness
$16.95 Cloth
The Staying Thin Program redesigned especially with kids and their families in mind. Doctor approved.

Available at fine bookstores everywhere
or directly from the publisher.

Nautilus Books, Inc.
496 LaGuardia Place, Suite 145
New York, NY 10012